Essays in
Modern Heathenry

Essays in Modern Heathenry

Galina Krasskova

Hubbardston, Massachusetts

Asphodel Press
12 Simonds Hill Road
Hubbardston, MA 01452

Essays in Modern Heathenry
© 2011 by Galina Krasskova
ISBN 978-0-615-26215-4

Printed in cooperation with
Lulu Enterprises, Inc.
860 Aviation Parkway, Suite 300
Morrisville, NC 27560

This book is dedicated to Alexei Kondratiev (1949-2010). Alexei was a good and gracious man. He was kind to me at a time when I was barely managing to do more than survive. He inspired me with my studies, and treated me as a colleague worthy of consideration in our many discussions. He always challenged me to go deeper into my studies and he was a damned fine Latin tutor. I credit him in large part with inspiring me to go into graduate work in Classics, and I wish that I had known him better.

I do know that he was a devotee of Brigid, one of Her shining flames: an author, a bard, and an amazing linguist. Not only did he speak all six Celtic languages, but Latin, ancient Greek, Hebrew, the romance languages—yes, all of them—Russian, and I believe, German. I asked him once how many languages, dialects included, that he spoke, and the man lost count at twenty. After his death, I found out that he spoke sixty-four, including several Native American languages. He also played a mean Celtic harp.

In addition to teaching Irish Gaelic, he worked hard trying to expand Celtic Reconstructionist religion (Imbas) into a living, burning faith, grounded in rigorous scholarship and the beauty and majesty of the Celtic languages. His book **The Apple Branch** *was, to my mind, ground-breaking.*

May the Gods welcome him home. May he join with pride the halls of his ancestors. May his name be hailed with pride by those who knew him and those who learned from him. Let us hail the passing of a good man and a great scholar. **Ave atque vale,** *most noble son of Brigid.*

Contents

Acknowledgements

Many thanks to Professor Wendi Wilkerson, PhD. for her kindness in vetting and proofing the final version of this manuscript. I deeply appreciate the time and hard work this entailed. Please be sure that any errors are entirely my own.

I would also like to thank (in no particular order) Raven Kaldera, Joshua Tenpenny, and Asphodel Press for their long-standing support, Mutti, Boo, K.C. Hulsman, Laura Patsouris, Dagara elders Rebecca DeGraw and Professor Ukumbwa Sauti, PhD., Elizabeth Vongvisith, my advisor for my first MA Professor Ann Pellegrini, PhD., Mercer Crenshaw (a man who kept me sane when I was doing that first Masters), S. Reicher, Professor H. Zimmerman, PhD., Hugette, Krei Steinberg (the best researcher in the business as well as a good and loyal friend), Michael Schütz and Michaela Macha, Queen Mother Imakhu, Trevor W. and his two friends who attended the CTCW conference in 2011 (you give me hope for the future of Heathenry), Linnie Hanna, Ursula Dabravalskas, Lola Garcia, all my Saxon boys, D. (aka: Pot), Sannion, Dver, Rebecca Buchanan, Alan Leddon, Peter Dybing (your work is an inspiration), Professor Sabina Magliocci, PhD., Mary Ann Glass, Allen Paiva, Kenaz, Kathy, and Annamaria Sigyn, and Anne Niven. Thank you all for your support.

Foreword

As the editor of *Huginn*, a biannual journal with the mandate of exploring alternative Heathen viewpoints, I have the opportunity to read a great deal of Heathen and Northern Tradition Pagan writing. Most of it is very thoughtful work from talented writers, a small fraction is highly bizarre, all of it is fascinating, and I value the privilege of curating these intimate and idiosyncratic portraits of people's practice.

A crucial part of living a religion—any religion—is being willing to get your hands dirty, to come down out of the ivory tower and figure out how the lofty concepts of religion actually integrate into real life. Ironically, I think, *Huginn* has taught me that most Heathens are well-engaged in the practical application; instead, I've ended up repeatedly lamenting (to those who will put up with it) that Heathenry is suffering from a scarcity of formal theologians. Not that it wants for academics, historians or scholars—indeed, ancient Scandinavian culture is more thoroughly documented than most European cultures—but virtually none of them are actually Heathen, practicing what they study. And as I said, Heathenry flourishes with active adherents who incorporate the gods, wights and ancestors into their daily lives. What Heathenry needs, I complained, are theologians who can do for the modern revival what Augustine or Aquinas did for the Church.

I met Galina Krasskova through *Huginn*; she is a rare asset to Heathenry, an academic who is nonetheless among the theological *innangard*. Besides being an indefatigable advocate for indigenous rights and the preservation of aboriginal culture, she is highly active within both Neo-Pagan and wider religious circles as both a scholar and a gythia. Galina is a very prolific author with a very practical approach to Heathenry; as well, she wins brownie points by authoring (currently) the only devotionals to Sigyn, for whom I also have a particular devotion. She's tremendously knowledgeable, and her writing speaks to years of practical experience, but most importantly—at least for this book—is her academic and seminarian background.

Galina's essays examine Heathenry in the context of not only the modern Neo-Pagan movement, but in the greater context of world religion. Of any scholar, she's the most uniquely placed to observe the parallels and contrasts between the Northern Tradition and other cultures. Her work stands in both the academic and religious spheres, and enriches both. Galina's also one of the most talented and pleasant writers I've had the pleasure to deal with through my work on *Huginn*. Christianity would certainly be intellectually poorer without its *patres ecclesiae*; modern Heathenry is still in its infancy and the revival has yet to be truly tested by time, but I am confident that we can count Galina among Heathenry's *matres religionis*.

TALAS PÁI
EDITOR, *HUGINN*
HTTP://WWW.HUGINNJOURNAL.COM
MARCH, 2012

Introduction: An Academic View of Heathenry

This book has taken me many years to write. First begun in 2005, it is a compilation of four academic articles, the outgrowth of many years of research which eventually culminated in a Master's degree in Religious Studies. I rarely have the opportunity to write as an academic. So much of my work within the community is focused on theology, teaching devotional consciousness, and reclaiming our indigenous traditions, while working within the academy is complicated by the fact that I am no unbiased outsider to the traditions (i.e., Heathenry) that I am researching. It puts me in a complicated place. At the same time, Heathenry has never (to date) been adequately addressed by the academy. That shouldn't be too surprising. Wicca is only now gaining some legitimacy within academic circles and in the US, even though it has been around in an organized form for a decade longer than any manifestation of Asatru or Heathenry. Moreover, too often academicians class Heathenry as a fringe religious movement with spurious ties to various and sundry white power movements. When Heathenry is addressed academically, it often happens only as a corollary to the latter, as in Gardell's *Gods of the Blood*. We have yet to see the type of serious scholarship within the field of Religious Studies exploring permutations of belief, praxis, and culture within Heathenry that religions like Islam or Christianity customarily warrant.

At the same time, Heathens themselves are loath to look at the sociopolitical context which first influenced the rise of American Asatru (the first manifestation of any branch of the Northern Tradition to spring up on US soil). Few Heathens are formally trained in the academic study of religion, as those who have graduate-level learning usually eschew Religious Studies for medieval history, and there has been no satisfactory examination of the social and cultural factors influencing certain ideological tropes in Heathenry until now. I hope to remedy that deficit with the book you now hold in your hands.

As I've already noted, I am not an unbiased observer of these cultural and religious currents. Not only have I been a practicing Heathen for close to twenty years, but I am quite likely the single most controversial Heathen writer and theologian currently in print. Nor am I writing from a place of purely academic interest. I care deeply about the future of Heathenry today. I care deeply about the restoration of Northern European indigeny; and, as anyone who has read any of my devotional work surely knows, I care deeply about seeing the rites and rituals by which our ancestors honored our Gods restored. That commitment stands hand in hand with my commitment to academic integrity. These articles have been meticulously researched and reflect my observations not only as a Heathen, but specifically as a Heathen academic of the salient issues affecting the community today.

I've chosen four articles for this book, each touching on a topic that I believe has had a major impact on the ideological fault lines currently raging within the American Heathen community. It should be noted that my research deals only with the American Heathen community (or perhaps *communities* would be far more accurate). These articles were written several years ago and it should also be noted that since the original time of writing, the controversies and attitudes encapsulated in these pages have grown to a fever-pitch. Heathenry is in the middle of a religious schism and with the articles in this book, I attempt to show exactly why.

The first article included here discusses cultural trends within the contemporary community, the beginnings of what anthropologist Pierre Bourdieu might have called *habitus*. Contemporary Heathenry, like many Reconstructionist Paganisms, is in the awkward position of forcing the development of its culture, something that is meant to develop organically and inter-generationally. There is an attendant self-consciousness inherent in the very process of restoration that complicates the development of an authentic indigenous consciousness—a necessary precursor, in my opinion, to any legitimate restoration.

The second article was first presented at an academic conference on Pagan Studies at Claremont Graduate University in California. It has also appeared in the journal *Huginn: A Journal of Alternative Heathen Viewpoints* and as part of the Pagan portal at patheos.com.

The third article discusses the confluence of three topics close to my heart: Odin, the ritual of *blót* and the importance of sacrifice within the Northern Tradition. It has often been asserted within the community that Heathenry is not a "mystery" religion. I would dispute that. Every indigenous tradition has its sacred mysteries. They may not have been open to every single person, but they existed. Even monotheistic religions have their mysteries. So this particular chapter begins the exploration of where our dominant mysteries might just lay. It's also an exploration of ritual dynamics, in particular the rite of sacrificial blot, at times a controversial practice in and of itself within Heathenry and certainly within the greater Pagan community. An earlier version of this article was originally presented at Harvard University's "Forging Folklore" colloquium in 2005.

The final article in this book explores the God Loki, at once the most intriguing and most vilified Deity in the Norse pantheon. Whether or not to honor Loki and His kin is perhaps the major ideological fault line within Heathenry today. Where one falls on this question alone can determine not only how one is received in various parts of the Heathen community, but whether or not one is even considered Heathen by the more conservative denominations. This chapter first appeared as an article both in *Huginn: A Journal of Alternative Heathen Viewpoints and at* patheos.com.

There is more to restoring a lost polytheism than simply exchanging one god for many. Truly rooting oneself in one's ancestral traditions, rebuilding cleanly and sustainably requires that we each essentially deprogram ourselves and change the ways in which we were taught to engage (or not engage) with the sacred. We are called to examine the filter, the lens through which we view the world, a lens put in place by the monotheistic culture in which we were raised—and American secularism is deeply informed by Protestant (and often fundamentalist) Christianity. That is difficult and challenging work. Heathenry is one of the fastest growing of contemporary Paganisms. Even as the community battles with itself, it is evolving. I believe that the questions I ask in my research—even if readers disagree with my conclusions—are questions that need to be asked in order to ensure that American Heathenry becomes strong. It is said that over the ancient Oracle of Delphi were carved words long considered a powerful maxim for those seeking wisdom amongst the ancient Greeks: ϒνῶθι σεαυτόν (Know Thyself). Good words. Good advice. It is equally important, as we move forward in this process of restoration that we too know ourselves and the origins of that which we are seeking to restore.

I hope in the coming years to see a generation of Heathen academics taking their place in the discipline of Religious Studies. That is part of reclaiming and restoring our indigenous traditions too – making sure that we are telling our own story, rather than allowing ourselves to be all-too-often ill-defined by others. This is my contribution to that work.

GALINA KRASSKOVA
DUTCHESS COUNTY NY
DECEMBER, 2011

The Development of Culture in Modern Heathenry

Imagine yourself standing in a grove of trees on a warm, sunny June day. The sun is almost directly overhead and there is a buzz of excitement in the air, belying the growing warmth of the day. All around you men and women stand gathered, nearly all dressed in puzzling garb. The men wear handcrafted tunics and trousers, many carefully embroidered with odd knotwork designs, and many have empty sheaths belted to their waists. The weapons lie carefully outside of the grove, and upon being asked about this oddity, one gentleman explains that iron weapons are tabooed on holy ground on this solstice day because of the pending sacrifice to Frey, God of the Earth. Some of the women wear sheaths at their waists too, but many more have donned the traditional "apron dresses" of a late Viking era Norse matron, complete with turtle brooches adorned with a remarkable array of hanging strands of polished amber[1]. Everyone's attention is directed to the center of the field where a small pen containing a healthy white pig lies.

Soon the priest enters the field, carrying a lit torch and chanting softly in old Anglo-Saxon while circling the ritual site. She too is dressed in Viking era clothing, but in her case, a substantial single-edged knife remains belted to her waist, and the long sleeves of her dress are tied carefully back. The prayers begin, some in modern English, some in old Anglo-Saxon, each hailing the God Frey as Lord of the land, thanking Him for His bounty. A large carved drinking horn is passed around the gathered folk and each person praises one of the Gods or Goddesses of the Norse pantheon and takes a drink. Folk are invited to go up and touch the pig, giving it messages to carry to the otherworld. Finally, at a sign from the priestess, two strong men bring the animal forward.

With spoken invocation to Frey, the priestess crouches down with her knife in hand. With a single, quick confident stroke, she slits the

---

[1] For those interested in Viking Age clothing styles, may I suggest the following link: <http://www.vikinganswerlady.com/clothing.shtml>.

animal's throat and captures the blood in a large wooden bowl. The animal dies without a sound, carrying the collected blessings of the people to their Gods and honored dead. Eventually the men take the animal away to begin the butchering process for the feast to follow. The priestess takes an evergreen branch and walking about the circle of her congregants, gently asperses each person with the collected blood of the sacrificial swine.

Thus is the reader introduced to one of the defining moments of Heathen religious culture: the sacrificial *blót*. Out of all the varying cultural and religious practices that are slowly coming to define this emergent faith, none highlight the differences between Heathenry and contemporary American cultures quite so glaringly as this particular rite, which is admittedly only performed by a very small minority of adherents[2]. Employing anthropologist Bronislaw Malinowski's ethnographic method in the beginning of this article has enabled me to highlight the strange cognitive disconnect that underlies the slow development of Heathen culture within the United States, a culture that is torn between the normative social and religious practices of ancient Scandinavia and the pressing pull of the modern world.[3] This chapter will address the issues and controversies inherent in the development of a normative religiously-based culture, and the intersection of both the sacred and secular within a modern American Heathen social context.

---

[2] As of 2006, 1/6 of 1% of modern Heathens practiced animal sacrifice, largely due to constraints of land, space and access to humanely raised livestock. (Krasskova, "Animal Sacrifice and the Ritual of *Blót* in Modern Heathenry: An Ethnographic Exploration." Presented May 5, 2007 at Harvard University's Forging Folklore Colloquium).

[3] Bronislaw Malinowski's work pioneered the functionalist school of anthropology, which holds that culture develops to meet deep-rooted personal needs rather than to meet the needs of a society's hierarchical structure. For further information, review Malinowski's *The Argonauts of the Western Pacific* (London: George Routledge and Sons, 1932).

Heathenry is a body of religious denominations sharing both a common pantheon and a core cultural cosmology. Practitioners are polytheists who worship (fairly exclusively) the Norse Gods and Goddesses. They are also Reconstructionists or, in some cases along the liberal end of the ideological spectrum, Reconstructionist-derived. The former believe in reconstructing religious and cultural practices of pre-Christian Scandinavia, Germany and/or England as accurately as possible making as few concessions as possible to the needs of modernity where belief and religious practice are concerned. The latter use the existing historical and literary material as a springboard for personal gnosis and grant such personal gnosis far greater weight in the development of religious and cultural norms. This is one of the primary ideological fault lines between varying denominations.

In writing about the people that he studied, anthropologist Bronislaw Malinowski occasionally chose to introduce his readers to the topic at hand with vignettes designed to draw the reader into a direct experience of the culture itself. By doing so, he provided a context for the explanation and analysis that would follow. Malinowski was a functionalist[4], meaning that he conceived of culture as being an inter-related series of practices, each of which in some way contributed to the stability of the society in which they developed. Such practices were, no matter how strange they might appear to outsiders' eyes, organic, functioning pieces of a greater cultural whole. In other words, within their culture of origin, specific practices and customs make sense. Nothing expresses cultural values more intrinsically than common religious practices. Emile Durkheim, in his seminal work *The Elementary Forms of Religious Life*, points out that:

> Religion is something eminently social. Religious representations are collective representations that express collective realities; rituals are ways of acting that

---

[4] Malinowski, *The Argonauts of the Western Pacific, 22.*

are generated only within assembled groups and are meant to stimulate and sustain or recreate certain mental states in these groups.[5]

Additionally, the definition of something so nebulous as "culture" or "religion" can be problematic in and of itself. Raymond Williams notes that "culture is one of the two or three most complicated words in the English language," largely because it has come to mean distinctly different things within the broad expanse of several distinctly different academic disciplines.[6] Religion of course, is no easier to define, particularly when we are examining the interstices between the two.

William Arnal writes that "no statement about what religion is can avoid at least partially explaining what religion does, where it comes from, and how it works."[7] This is an issue not just for the specialist, but for would-be theologians within the Asatru community as well. There is, especially given the rising denominational clashes within the religion, no fully accepted consensus on any of those things.

Leaving aside questions of definition, I believe it is possible to determine several clearly delineated factors within Heathenry, points of practice and approach (be they openly acknowledged or otherwise within the community) that most adherents would agree are uniquely Heathen. Individual communities possess their own unique cultures, often centered around and growing out of the common focus of people's collective experiences. In other words we have workplace culture, religious culture, even one's own family culture. Each of these cultures may possess their own special language, customs and rituals. This is why Durkheim, in writing about religion, noted that "religious beliefs proper are

---

[5] Emile Durkheim, *The Elementary Forms of Religious Life* (Oxford: Oxford University Press, 2001), 11.

[6] Raymond Williams, *Keywords* (New York: Oxford University Press, 1983), 87.

[7] William Arnal, "Definition" in *Guide to the Study of Religion* (London: Cassell, 2000), 22.

always held by a *defined* collectivity *[emphasis mine]* that professes them and practices the rites that go with them."[8]

To be sure, there has been some very tentative work done within the Heathen community on just this subject. Dr. Stephen Flowers (a.k.a. Edred Thorsson), in an article published in the journal *Tyr: Myth, Culture, Tradition* discusses the idea of Heathen culture by dividing it into four categories: ethnic, ethical, material, and linguistic.[9] He goes on to explain that "symbolic, or ethical, culture is entirely invisible and supersensible. We know about it through its manifestations in the other three branches of culture: ethnic, material, and linguistic."[10]

So what are these unspoken cultural markers? Flowers postulates that culture is most perfectly encoded in the linguistic code utilized within a given community. and within the Heathen community this certainly holds true.[11] The Heathen communities utilize a very specific language with many terms drawn from Old Norse or Old English to define ideology and to bracket their communal experience. They also use these same terms in an exclusionary fashion when questions of difference in practice arise. Among these rather charged terms are: *Frið*, *Grið*, Hospitality, and *Recht*.

Frið is an Old Norse word that indicates "right order" or "right balance" between friends. In the community, it is used to indicate the state of harmony and peace that exists in a cohesive community, peace enjoyed while amongst one's own people. The unspoken reality about the use of the term *frið* within modern Heathenry is that it has come to assume a presupposed homogeneity within any given group, a homogeneity of thought and values, of both orthodoxy and orthopraxy, which can and has

---

[8] Durkheim, *The Elementary Forms of Religious Life*, 42.

[9] Stephen Edred Flowers, "The Idea of Integral Culture: A Model for a Revolt Against the Modern World." in *Tyr: Myth, Culture, Tradition vol.* 1, ed. Joshua Buckley (Atlanta: Ultra Press, 2002), 12.

[10] Ibid., 13.

[11] Ibid., 13.

led to a division between *inangarð* (the sacred enclosure of one's community) and *utgarð* (everyone else).

Grið, perhaps best understood as the other side of *frið*, is the state of détente between members of an *inangarð* and members of an *utgarð*; such as when visitors from another denomination may visit and participate in one group's religious celebrations or feasts. The use of this term in online forums within the community highlights the almost xenophobic insularity that has come to define certain aspects of Heathen practice, most particularly within the orthodox community.

Hospitality, as understood in Heathenry, is the open-handed generosity with which members of the community are expected to treat each other and visitors. The idea of hospitality is spoken of quite frequently in inter-Heathen discourse and it is held up as a high ideal within every branch of the greater Heathen community. At its best, the ideal of hospitality leads to a cohesive, supportive infrastructure upon which Heathen leaders can build. At its worst, visitors and long-term Heathens who express dissent with the commonly accepted orthodoxy can be met with open hostility and suspicion, as even the most cursory exploration of the online Heathen community will show.

Recht, a concept taken from the German word for "right," is used primarily by the Theodish—a Heathen sub-community that, in the last five years, has gained a tremendous amount of influence within greater Heathenry—when discussing the hermeneutics of practice and the evolving Heathen Weltanschauung. This goes hand in hand with a certain romanticizing of pre-Christian Heathen cultures due to the belief, in the words of Theodish leader Daniel O'Halloran, that:

> [W]e have been stripped for over a millennia of our cultural and religious values, and the world has, for the most part, suffered under a Judeo-Christian paradigm. That paradigm has for the most part, repressed our faith, contradicted our

worldview, and attempted to trivialize, destroy or hide anything that once composed the elder religious systems of the World.[12]

O'Halloran goes on to note that "Asatru tends to work backwards from the modern period, incorporating elements of the elder culture through the religion as understood today" whereas "Theodism tends to work forward from the elder period and incorporate elements of modern culture where they are compatible with what would be regarded as lawful (or *recht*) in elder times."[13]

O'Halloran's comments regarding the "elder period" of Heathenry aptly illustrate the religion's ongoing attempts to create what Fabian termed "intersubjective Time" between modern adherents and pre-Christian believers in the same set of Gods.[14] There is an overwhelming desire, openly stated in many parts of the community, to develop Heathenry and by extension Heathen culture as though the intervening millennia of Christianity had never occurred. In his work *Time and the Other*, Fabian discusses the idea of time as a device used to create (or in some cases deny) coevalness. This idea of coevalness, a sharing of present time, is precisely what the Heathen community is trying to create with its interpretations of the past. This holds forth positively in the ancestral veneration which is an important part of the religion, but also in the developing aesthetic as well as (and most importantly to our discussion) the developing attitudes and value judgments that define the religion. Moreover, the way in which most Heathens approach their religious culture depends heavily on the sense of deep connectedness to their "shared" past with its attendant values and culture. The development of a sense of

---

[12] From a public email on the <northeastasatru@yahoogroups.com> mailing list by Mr. O'Halloran, October 6, 2007, message #19350).

[13] Ibid.

[14] Johannes Fabian, *Time and the Other: How Anthropology Makes Its Object* (New York: Columbia University Press, 2002), 42.

coevalness ceases to be a problem for the modern Heathen; rather, it is presupposed.

Curiously, one aspect of this *Weltanschauung* is the nearly blanket denial within large swaths of the Heathen community that Norse cultures were ever seriously influenced by any external factors prior to the arrival of Christianity. Despite the remarkably advanced system of trade that defined the Viking world, Heathen purists persist in insisting that neither the Celtic nor the Saami nor the Finnish nor any Mediterranean cultures had any lasting or important influence on the development of Norse magico-religious traditions, and that there was never any blending of practice. This attitude of adamant insularity permeates not just Heathen attitudes toward the past, but also their attitude toward the development of the modern religion. Any influences not immediately attested to in "the lore", be they religious, cultural or even aesthetic, are met with deep hostility, including many aspects of personal gnosis. This includes not just religious practices such as certain kinds of prayer and meditation, but also ritual clothing styles, iconography, gender roles and religious eclecticism. It has contributed in a large part, as we shall later see, to the development of a rather exclusionary and xenophobic attitude within the greater community.

Essentially, modern Heathenry has created what anthropologist Johannes Fabian warns researchers not to do: they have taken both Nordic cultures and modern Heathen cultures and created the religious equivalent of a "culture garden". This has had the unfortunate effect of trapping the developing modern culture like a bee in amber, slowing down its evolution and fettering it to an idealized concept of the past that rarely if ever actually existed. In many respects, this has locked Heathenry away not only from external influences of other religions, but also from the evolutionary trends slowly gaining momentum within fringe elements of the greater Heathen community itself. Above all else, by bounding Heathenry off from dialogue with not only the greater Neo-Pagan communities but also the different denominations within Heathenry itself, it has created a rigid, exclusionary border across which newcomers to the faith find it very difficult to pass. It has effectively made a weapon of Heathen culture.

Bibliography

Arnal, William. "Definition." *Guide to the Study of Religion*, Eds., Willi Braun and Russell T. McCutcheon. London: Cassell, 2000. 21-34.

Durkheim, Emile. *The Elementary Forms of Religious Life*. Oxford: Oxford University Press, 2002.

Fabian, Johannes. *Time and the Other: How Anthropology Makes Its Object*. New York: Columbia University Press. 2002.

Flowers, Stephen. "The Idea of Integral Culture: A Model for a Revolt Against the Modern World." *Tyr: Myth, Culture, Tradition* vol. 1 2002, ed. Joshua Buckley. Atlanta: Ultra Press. pp. 11-22.

Krasskova, Galina. *Exploring the Northern Tradition*. New Jersey: New Page Books, 2005.

Magliocco, Sabina. *Witching Culture*. Philadelphia: University of Pennsylvania Press, 2004.

Malinowski, Branislaw. *The Argonauts of the Western Pacific*. London: George Routledge and Sons, 1932.

Williams, Raymond. *Keywords*. New York: Oxford University Press, 1983.

Performativity and the Development of Modern Heathen Culture

Contemporary Northern Tradition Paganism or Heathenry is a body of religions in the midst of tremendous flux. Since 2006, ideological debates over theology, self-definition, and the role of personal gnosis in general and liminal practices in particular (including but not limited to ecstatic mysticism, Deity possession, shamanism, and even such common activities as prayer and devotional practice) have come to dominate public discourse within these religions.[1] This ongoing discourse has served to highlight the major ideological fault line within Heathenry articulated by Heathen author Fuensanta Plaza: the conflict between a body of scholarship that Heathens term "the lore"[2] and the validity of personal gnosis.[3] At the heart of this battle lies a deeper issue: the power of the actual performance of religious rituals in transforming the structure, accepted orthodoxy, and

---

[1] 2006 saw the performance of a ritual *blót* (sacrificial rite) that included the sacrifice of a sheep to the Goddess Angrboda. Angrboda is one of a family of Gods called the *Jotnar*, who are associated with primal power, chaos and destructive forces. Whether or not They should be honored within the modern religion is a point of intense controversy and contention. The performance of this *blót* and the following public accounts of the experience brought this particular ideological controversy out into the open in a way that has, in this author's opinion, polarized the community. This year also saw the publication of a very controversial book advocating worship of the *Jotnar* and replete with personal gnosis: *Jotunbok: Working with the Giants of the Northern Tradition* by Raven Kaldera (Massachusetts: Asphodel Press, 2006).

[2] "Lore", as Heathens define it, is comprised of the Poetic Edda, Prose Edda, the Icelandic Sagas, any extant historical, legal, medical or magical writings from Scandinavia, England or Germany up through the conversion, combined with modern scholarship in a plethora of fields from linguistics to history, archaeology to folklore. The majority of these sources were written down at least two hundred years after the conversion of Iceland and none of them were ever consciously intended to be utilized as religious scripture. See also Chapter Nine in *Northern Tradition for the Solitary Practitioner* by Galina Krasskova Krasskova and Raven Kaldera (New Jersey: New Page Books, 2009).

[3] Fuensanta Plaza, personal correspondence with author, April 10, 2008.

ritual expectations within this body of religions. This article will explore the impact of ritual performance on the development of devotional practices and mystical traditions within the greater Northern Tradition. It will also examine the influence of such performativity on the aforementioned primary ideological fault line within Heathenry—the authority of written sources versus the authority of personal gnosis.

At the time of this writing, there has been almost nothing written within the academy about modern Heathenry. The three exceptions to this are *Gods of the Blood* by Mattias Gardell[4], an article by Michael Strmiska that appeared in the October 2000 issue of *Nova Religio* titled "Ásatru in Iceland: The Rebirth of Nordic Paganism?",[5] and a chapter based on that article which subsequently appeared in Strmiska's *Modern Paganism.*[6] The first examines Folkish Heathenry, the minority branch of the religion that emphasizes ethnicity and blood lines and its sometime connection to white separatism. The latter article and follow-up book chapter examine the growth of Heathenry in Iceland, where it has been named (as of 1973) the second state religion. Heathen ritual dynamics and their influence on the development of orthodoxy have yet to be explored at all, be it in academic or popular press.

Throughout this chapter, I utilize Pierre Bourdieu's theories of habitus, ritual, and bodily hexis to frame my argument that it is the active performance of ritual that has not only transformed the American Heathen community, but also challenged the very

---

[4] Mattias Gardell, *Gods of the Blood* (Philadelphia: University of Pennsylvania Press, 2003).

[5] Michael Strmiska, "Ásatrú in Iceland: The Rebirth of Nordic Paganism?" Nova Religio 4, no. 1 (2000): 106–132.

[6] Michael Strmiska and Baldur A Sigurvinsson, "Asatru: Nordic Paganism in Iceland and America." in *Modern Paganism in World Cultures: Comparative Perspectives* ed. Michael Strmiska (New York: ABC-CLIO, 2005).

foundations upon which its dominant orthodoxies are based.[7] In *Outline of a Theory and Practice* Bourdieu writes:

> Understanding ritual practice is not a question of decoding the internal logic of a symbolism but of restoring its practical necessity by relating it to the real conditions of its genesis, that is, to the conditions in which it functions, and the means it uses to attain them, are defined.[8]

Essentially, the body itself is not just something upon which politics and theology happens; rather, the body is a means of registering the world without verbalizing. Ritual is an extension of that experience. Bourdieu further notes that:

> Rites take place because and only because they find their *raison d'être* in the conditions of existence and the dispositions of agents who cannot afford the luxury of logical speculation, mystical effusions, or metaphysical anxiety.[9]

In other words, rites and rituals can establish mimetic relationships between objects, processes, and key elements of the cosmology, but at the same time, they can also challenge those self-same structures. Within Heathenry, the ritual structure is largely predicated on extant accounts found in the Icelandic sagas. One of the most thorough descriptions of a ritual involving sacrifice can be found in Snorri Sturluson's *Heimskringla*:

---

[7] Throughout this chapter, any reference to Heathenry, Asatru, or the Northern Tradition refers only to the American communities. The issues and controversies that frame the European and Icelandic communities are, in many cases, completely different.

[8] Pierre Bourdieu, *Outline of a Theory of Practice* (Cambridge: Cambridge University Press, 2007), 214.

[9] Ibid., 115.

It was an old custom, that when there was to be sacrifice, all the *bondes* should come to the spot where the temple stood and bring with them all that they required while the festival of the sacrifice lasted. To this festival all the men brought ale with them; and all kinds of cattle, as well as horses, were slaughtered, and all the blood that came from them was called *hlaut*, and the vessels in which it was collected were called *hlaut*-vessels. *Hlaut*-staves were made, like sprinkling brushes, with which the whole of the altars and the temple walls, both outside and inside, were sprinkled over, and also the people were sprinkled with the blood; but the flesh was boiled into savoury meat for those present. The fire was in the middle of the floor of the temple, and over it hung the kettles, and the full goblets were handed across the fire; and he who made the feast, and was a chief, blessed the full goblets, and all the meat of the sacrifice. And first Odin's goblet was emptied for victory and power to his king; thereafter, Niord's and Freyja's goblets for peace and a good season. Then it was the custom of many to empty the *brage*-goblet;[10] and then the guests emptied a goblet to the memory of departed friends, called the remembrance goblet.[11]

The contemporary Heathen ritual of *symbel* follows this format almost precisely, making as few accommodations as they

---

[10] The *Braga-full* over which vows and sacred oaths were made. This has survived in the modern heathen practice of *symbel* (or *sumbel*) in which a horn filled with alcohol is passed around three times: once to honor the Gods, once to honor ancestors and once to make sacred vows or boasts. A vow taken over the horn is especially sacred within Heathen tradition.

[11] "Hakon the Good's Saga" from *Heimskringla* by Snorri Sturluson. The excerpt here is taken from a version published by the Norroena Society, London, 1907. This version may be found online at:
<www.northvegr.org/lore/heim/index.html>.

believe necessary to modernity, and the format of other standard rituals within modern Heathenry is largely drawn from descriptions such as this one found in the Icelandic Sagas and other first and second hand sources of the time.

In addition to Bourdieu, Sabina Magliocco's study of folklore and contemporary Neo-Paganism provides useful background information in the examination of the constituent demographic of contemporary Heathenry, particularly with respect to the dominant Protestant *Weltanschauung* that so informs modern Northern Tradition orthodoxy[12]. Saba Mahmood's insights on the influence and development of invented traditions, drawn from her work on the *dawa* movement in Egypt also help to elaborate the conflicting tensions defining Heathenry today. Mahmood, in her discussion of issues surrounding embodied practices and invented traditions notes:

> Scholarly arguments are not simply frozen bodies of texts, but live through the discursive practices of both lettered and unlettered Muslims whose familiarity with these arguments is grounded in a variety of sources – not all of which are controlled by scholars.[13]

While Mahmood's work *Politics of Piety* focuses exclusively on Islam—specifically Egyptian women's involvement in preaching and religious education—her insights into the way in which active performance of a faith can contribute to the development of that faith and its prevailing orthodoxies, despite resistance from the formal purveyors of that orthodoxy are particularly applicable within the frame of contemporary Heathenry as well.

---

[12] Sabina Magliocco, *Witching Culture* (Philadelphia: University of Pennsylvania Press, 2004).

[13] Saba Mahmood, *Politics of Piety* (Princeton, NJ: Princeton University Press, 2005), 96.

It is difficult to speak of any one Heathen community. The Northern Tradition, for which the umbrella term "Heathenry" is the chosen identity of choice for the majority of adherents, is comprised of many different denominations and ideological approaches. It is far more accurate to refer to the Northern Tradition as being comprised of multiple communities that simply happen to share a common core cosmology. Approach and belief surrounding that cosmology may be dramatically and often radically different between denominations, particularly within the United States.

There are two primary ritual structures within the contemporary Northern Tradition, and these structures are shared by nearly every denomination: *blót*, which may or may not include animal sacrifice depending on the denomination, and *symbel*. Only Norse Paganism and Northern Tradition shamanism, both of which define themselves as Reconstructionist-derived (meaning that their adherents utilize the surviving lore as a "jumping off point" to personal gnosis) rather than strict Reconstructionist, practice other forms of ritual, often incorporating experiential and even ecstatic ritual elements.[14]

The most common ritual of all is the *blót*. The most insular and orthodox (in that they hold to a very strict interpretation of lore, hierarchical social structure and rigid gender boundaries) denomination, called Theodism, utilizes the term *blót* only for those rituals involving animal sacrifice. Any other offering rite is called a *faining*. Outside of Theodism, however, the term *blót* is utilized for any offering rite, whether or not actual blood sacrifice is present. The format of the basic *blót* is simple:

❖ The folk gather and the space is hallowed.
❖ The Gods and/or Goddesses are invoked and all the offerings are blessed.

---

[14] Raven Kaldera, personal correspondence with author, March 31, 2008.

❖ A horn of alcohol, usually mead is passed around and each person individually hails the Deities in question.

❖ If the rite includes animal sacrifice, it occurs at this point and congregants are aspersed with the animal's blood. If it does not, the remaining alcohol is poured out into a blessing bowl, the Gods are thanked and the offerings poured out in the appropriate place.

❖ The rite is then closed by prayer or blessing song. A feast may follow the *blót*, particularly if an animal is sacrificed. It is almost inevitably shared amongst the congregants in a sacred feast.

In the huge majority of groups, the sacrificial *blót* takes the form of pouring large quantities of mead and alcohol out in offering. Cooked (not sacrificed) food may be offered to both the Gods and ancestors and occasionally as in antiquity, domestic items, jewelry and weapons are given. Within the structure of a *blót,* extemporaneous expressions of devotion, including impassioned prayer, are not encouraged.[15]

The second ritual commonly practiced within the Northern Tradition is that of *symbel*. This is a community-building rite that does not commonly include offerings to the Gods. Instead, the community members gathered around a table and a horn or cup of alcohol is passed around the table at least three times. In the first round, congregants hail their ancestors as ancestral veneration is a very important part of the Northern Tradition; in the second round, the Gods and Goddesses are hailed; and in the third round, gifts may be exchanged cementing both bonds and hierarchy within the community, oaths may be taken, people may boast about deeds they have accomplished or wish to accomplish, and ancestors or Gods may be hailed again. Here, extemporaneous

---

[15] Fuensanta Plaza, personal correspondence with author, April 20, 2008.

expressions of community bonding, gregariousness, and—to a certain limited degree—devotion are considered appropriate.[16]

In order to better understand ritual dynamics and expectations within contemporary Heathenry it is necessary to understand the dominant factors driving the cultural development and expression within this body of religions. Heathenry, like other contemporary Reconstructionist Paganisms, is unique in that it is self-consciously attempting to reconstruct an ancient tradition drawing largely on extant historical sources. There is an unacknowledged tension within the communities between this conscious reconstruction and what may be the first stirrings of organic evolution. As people have been practicing the actual religions for over twenty years, slowly but surely there has been the beginning of a shift in what determines the religions' evolution. For the first fifteen years or so it was solely concentrated on the study of "lore". As more and more attention has been given to actual ritual practice, the Gods have become a far more important idea within the religion; by extension the past decade has seen a growing desire to develop devotional practices external to what has been recorded in the extant historical documents—which is to say, almost nothing at all.

This has caused great conflict within Heathenry as a whole, particularly in the United States.[17] The actual embodied practice of rituals like *blót* has had the startling and quite unexpected result of moving the religion ever so slowly away from textual authority by virtue of the power of the experience. Essentially, as people begin to actually practice a religion instead of solely studying its history and structure, it becomes impossible to predict where the experience of the sacred will lead them. This tension mirrors the developing ideological fault line currently threatening to tear the community apart: the aforementioned battle between the

---

[16] Fuensanta Plaza, personal correspondence with author, April 20, 2008.

[17] Elizabeth Vongvisith, personal communication with author, March 3, 2008.

authority of written sources and the often suspect authority of personal gnosis.

Modern Heathenry is a religion largely defined by its hermeneutics. A staunchly conservative community, modern Heathens—regardless of denomination—look to "lore" to define the structure and practice of their beliefs. "Lore" is comprised of the surviving Icelandic Sagas, Anglo-Saxon medical and legal texts, Germanic folk tales, *Poetic Edda, Prose Edda,* and any all historical documentation or studies. While none of these texts hold the authority within this religion that the Koran holds for Muslims or the Bible for Christians, at the same time these writings are accorded definite weight and carry great normative authority in determining the evolution of religious practice and accepted ideology within the faith.

The community by and large resists the development of any overarching theodicy, and mystical participation in religious life is viewed at best with suspicion. *UPG*—unverified personal gnosis— is treated with, if not open hostility, then at best with suspicion unless it conforms to the boundaries defined by the "lore".[18] This affects every aspect of Heathen ritual and religious life, and though a countermovement is slowly gaining momentum within the community, to date "lore" holds sway above any legitimacy of personal experience. Personal gnosis is devalued not only because it is unverifiable by the existing sources but because it rests on experience, emotion, and non-rational subjectivity. In espousing personal and direct experience with the Gods it also presumes an authority that clearly circumvents normative human mores. As noted above, this is the site of *the* major ideological fault line

---

[18] The term "UPG" first appeared in print in Kaatryn MacMorgan's 2003 publication *Wicca 333: Advanced Topics in Wiccan Belief* (Bloomington, IN: iUniverse). The term has since been widely adopted by people seeking deeper and less conventional relationships with the divine. Further adumbrations of the UPG concept such as those mentioned here have become part of contemporary polytheist and Pagan oral traditions.

within Heathenry. It is possible to determine denomination by which side of the debate over "lore" vs. "UPG" one falls.[19]

Some modern Heathens of a more ecumenical persuasion have theorized that perhaps this rigid adherence to lore alone is a reaction to the historically inaccurate practices of many Wiccans and other Neo-Pagans, with whom Heathenry is often (to their minds) incorrectly classified. Others have theorized that since Heathenry is a religion of converts primarily (only now is the second generation being born and raised into the faith), these converts carry with them a tendency toward fundamentalism not only as a way of defining themselves within their new faith, but perhaps out of unexamined ideological indoctrination from their birth religions, usually Protestant Christianity.[20]

There is no evidence that the pre-Christian worshippers of the Germanic Gods possessed the ideological xenophobia that so characterizes modern Heathenry, particularly the more restrictive and "orthodox" denominations. In fact, there is compelling evidence that, like the Paganisms of ancient Rome, the Germanic tribes had an accepting, if not ecumenical attitude toward different religions. According to Thomas Dubois, the scholarship of recent decades confirms a far more culturally interconnected worldview of Viking Age Europe between the Anglo-Saxons, Balto-Finnic, Celtic, Saami and Norse cultures.[21] Furthermore, there would have been no need for such orthodoxy: the religion was not in opposition to the dominant culture. The initial attitude toward foreign Gods was quite likely not hostile. The difference is that any religion they came in contact with prior to the advent of

---

[19] Galina Krasskova, *Exploring the Northern Tradition* (New Jersey: New Page Books, 2005), 12-14.

[20] While no formal studies have been done, it is an acknowledged fact within the community that the majority of members converted from Protestant often fundamentalist denominations. Among more liberal groups, there has been the occasional conversation on the manner in which this impacts ritual construction and expectations, but this awareness is not widespread.

[21] Thomas Dubois, *Nordic Religions in the Viking Age* (Philadelphia: University of Pennsylvania Press, 1999), 12-28.

Christianity would have been grounded in the specific cultures of its adherents providing a logical continuity of cosmological understanding. Such religions would only become a threat once their dogmatic imperative became the dissolution and destruction of other beliefs.[22]

As Ann Pellegrini and Janet Jakobson note in *Love the Sin,* "the dominant framework for morality [within the United States] is not simply 'religious' or even 'Christian,' but is specifically Protestant."[23] While Heathenry draws heavily on antique sources for its inspiration, those self-same sources were, with few exceptions, actually written well after Europe's conversion to Christianity. There has been almost no examination of the possible "Christianization" of these elder sources within Heathenry.

Northern Tradition shaman Raven Kaldera, in commenting on the influence of Christian values on modern Heathenry, notes:

> Most Heathens are coming into Heathenry with Christian values, and the familiar values that they seize upon from the cultural writings are the Christian ones, not the Pagan ones. The older Pagan faiths were not generally a source of moral values as these were drawn from the respective cultures instead. Modern Reconstructionist Pagans, having been raised expecting to be able to go to their religions for a clear list of moral rules, find themselves in a quandary when they are suddenly practicing a religion outside of the culture in which it evolved. Instead of examining and picking apart the writings of lore and separating Christian from Pagan influences, they fixate on what is familiar.[24]

---

[22] Krasskova, *Exploring the Northern Tradition*, 18.

[23] Janet Jakobson and Ann Pellegrini, *Love the Sin* (Boston: Beacon Press, 2004), 22.

[24] Raven Kaldera, personal communication with author, April 15, 2008.

For religious scholar Richard King, religion involves "retracing of 'the lore of the ritual' of one's ancestors."[25] The pre-Christian definition of religion, or *religio,* involved proper ritual practices and proper offerings to the Gods. It did not involve a clearly defined and mandated morality. There was no concept of such practices being true or false on a moral level. As King further notes:

> One could ask if one was faithfully adhering to a particular ancestral practice but one could not discuss its truth or falsity without fundamentally misunderstanding the nature of *religio* and *tradition.*[26]

It is precisely this understanding of religion that is absent in contemporary Heathen theology.

Modern Heathen or Asatru culture is a culture suspended between ever-changing and often conflicting social and religious axes.[27] Adherents to this body of religions are involved in the self-conscious reconstruction of a theology and body of social practices that developed in Northern Europe before the coming of Christianity. These contemporary Pagans must tackle the conundrum of attempting to reconstruct a religion in a culture radically different from the one in which that religion initially evolved. The development not only of religious orthodoxy but also of a coherent, homogenous "folkway" is of utmost importance within nearly every branch of this religion.[28] Subtle (and sometimes not so subtle) social pressure is often placed on

---

[25] Richard King, *Orientalism and Religion* (London: Routledge, 2005), 35.

[26] Ibid., 37.

[27] Asatru is the largest denomination within the United States.

[28] "Folkway" is a term that has come into common usage within the Heathen community to indicate the organic fusion of culture and social structure in addition to religion. It is not uncommon to read posts in online Heathen forums wherein the writer comments that Heathenry is "more than just a religion, it's a folkway". It is not known where this term developed.

practitioners to adhere to *thew* or unspoken cultural rules in a manner that is seen as acceptable to the majority.[29]

Nothing expresses cultural values more intrinsically than common religious practices. Emile Durkheim, in his seminal work *The Elementary Forms of Religious Life*, points out that:

> Religion is something eminently social. Religious representations are collective representations that express collective realities; rituals are ways of acting that are generated only within assembled groups and are meant to stimulate and sustain or recreate certain mental states in these groups.[30]

Asatru, or Heathen culture is fundamentally focused around creating a culture of the sacred that utilizes those commonly shared religious concepts to define their *social* identity. This ongoing process of religio-cultural synthesis presents the researcher with several unique difficulties, perhaps the most pressing of which is that there is no clear agreement amongst Asatruar about what precisely constitutes the clear boundaries of their community or the culture they seek to create. Indeed many would argue that there is not any such thing as "Asatru culture"; only to follow that statement by describing several clearly defined cultural markers by which they recognize themselves and others as Heathen.[31]

Realistically, when examining the growth and development of a Heathen culture (or cultures, given the often extreme

---

[29] *Thew* is a word commonly used in American Heathenry, particularly in orthodox Theodism, which is the most hierarchical and socially rigid branch of the religion, to mean tribal or communal law and/or custom. These are not laws that are written down but rather are understood from exposure to and integration into the community's *Weltanschauung*.

[30] Emile Durkheim, *The Elementary Forms of Religious Life* (Oxford: Oxford University Press, 2001), 11.

[31] Brian Smith, personal communication with author, September 9, 2007.

denominational differences) it is also necessary to study the dominant cultural paradigm from which the majority of modern Heathens are coming—in other words, 20th century North American culture, and specifically North American religious culture. The reality of modern American Asatru is that not only is it still a religion predominantly of converts but the overwhelming majority of those converts come from working- to middle-class Protestantism.[32] This latter fact is particularly important when one examines the expectations the majority of Heathens have regarding their religious culture and the rituals that define it.

In her study of modern Neo-Paganism, *Witching Culture*, anthropologist Sabina Magliocco discusses this particular aspect of Heathen culture. In an interview with priest Laurel Olson, one of the women responsible for helping to begin the reconstruction of Heathen oracular and magico-religious practices in the United States, this exact issue comes to light. Dr. Magliocco, in speaking of Ms. Olson, notes:

> She believes that Heathenism appeals to them [Heathens] because of its textual basis in the Norse and Icelandic sagas and the Eddas—a textual focus that recalls the biblical literalism already familiar to them through their birth religions. She also remarked on the formal, rather staid nature of many Heathen rituals, relating it to their general discomfort with loss of control and expression of emotion.[33]

This, perhaps more than any other factor, has dramatically impacted the development of this religious culture and the expectations of its adherents, as evidenced by the growing schism within the religion between the majority who accept the textually based orthodoxy and those who seek to grant moral supremacy or

---

[32] Raven Kaldera, personal communication with author, April 5, 2008.

[33] Sabina Magliocco, *Witching Culture* (Philadelphia: University of Pennsylvania Press, 2004), 77.

at the very least equal weight to mystical gnosis, moving beyond the normative authority of a written body of lore.

It should be noted that these written materials constituting Heathen "lore" (the Poetic and Prose Eddas, Icelandic sagas, Anglo Saxon histories and legal codes, Icelandic legal codes, historical, anthropological and linguistic work) were *never* intended to be utilized as religious material. The *Poetic Edda*, the primary text utilized by contemporary Heathens, was written in the 13th century, two hundred years after Iceland had already converted. It was written by Christian politician and statesman Snorri Sturluson largely as an aid toward the training of skalds and poets.

This emphasis on textual sources is common to all Reconstructionist Paganisms, yet it is particularly dominant within the Northern Tradition.[34] In speaking of Hellenismos, the reconstruction of ancient Greek polytheism, Drew Campbell notes:

> An important note on sources: Scholarship and intellectual honesty are very important to us, and Reconstructionists of all types emphasize the importance of distinguishing carefully between different sources of knowledge. In particular, we tend to be very critical of those who attempt to pass off personal gnosis as ancient fact or who make historical claims for which they cannot provide any hard evidence.[35]

---

[34] Reconstructionist Paganisms like Heathenry, Romuva (Baltic Paganism), Hellenismos (Greek Paganism), etc. use the term Reconstructionist because of their focus on reconstructing pre-Christian beliefs. It is this author's belief that the term is also used to differentiate themselves from eclectic Neo-Paganisms, religions that do not have such a historical or textual focus.

[35] Drew Campbell, "About Hellenismos" on Ecauldron.com, <http://www.ecauldron.com/dc-faq.php>

It is nearly impossible to study Heathen culture without also examining this earlier, formative influence. Like many Fundamentalist sects of Christianity, Heathenry in general believes very strongly that their beliefs are outside of the dominant culture's norms. While it is unlikely that many modern Heathens, with their emphasis on self-reliance (enshrined in a common Heathen ethical code called the Nine Noble Virtues) would admit to it, this attitude points to a certain feeling of alienation.[36] Dan O'Halloran, head of Normanni Theod, part of the ultra orthodox denomination of Theodism comments on just this when he says[37]:

> For better or ill 2007 is a time wherein we have been stripped for over a millennia (maybe two) of our cultural and religious values, and the world has, for the most part, suffered under a Judeo-Christian paradigm. That paradigm has for the most part repressed our faith, contradicted our world view, and attempted to trivialize, destroy, or hide anything that once composed the elder religious systems of the world. It is hard to understand, let alone envisage, the world as our ancestors did largely because of the impact of the Judeo-Christian (post-Roman) worldview that underlies everything from our concepts of time, to right and wrong, morality, existence, self worth, and to even the afterlife.[38]

---

[36] The Nine Noble Virtues are an ethical code common to most denominations of Heathenry. The virtues are courage, honor, hospitality, discipline, industriousness, self-reliance, truth, perseverance, and fidelity.

[37] Theodish Heathens often define themselves as orthodox. This denomination of Heathenry espouses rigid gender roles and hierarchical social structure, and focuses on a literal interpretation of the lore in as much as is possible. They are also possessed of an extremely binary view of the Gods: Aesir and Vanir are, in their world view, positive forces and in nearly all cases, the Jotnar are "evil".

[38] Dan O'Halloran, posting to the <northeastasatru@yahoogroups.com> discussion list, October 6, 2007.

This sense of alienation from the dominant cultural paradigm that so pervades the Heathen community has led to a fervent desire across nearly all denominational lines to see the development not only of Heathen religion, but also of an abiding tradition that will outlast the current generation as a single, powerful and most importantly homogenous whole. Adherents largely see themselves as actively engaged in the process of building a community, a culture and a tradition. There may be no clear-cut consensus on what these attendant cultural markers are, but there is a heated desire to have them. There is also a pervasive sense that this budding tradition needs to be protected both from outsiders and from those *within the community* who may hold alternate views:

> Indigenous cultures do not generally allow outsiders free access to the Mysteries. We need to emulate the American Indians and other groups, enforcing what I call "a holy reserve" in regard to the Sacred. That which is open to all is respected by none.[39]

Bourdieu wrote that "tradition is silent, not the least about itself as a tradition." [40] Ironically, as the Heathen communities battle vociferously online and in person for control over the direction in which their tradition should develop, it is already developing around them.

Secondly, an overwhelming majority of the Heathen demographic within the United States came to Heathenry in part due to an attraction to or admiration for not only the Gods of Heathenry, but also what Stephen McNallen, one of the founding

---

[39] Joshua Buckley, *Tyr: Myth, Culture, Tradition vol. 1 and 2* (Atlanta: Ultra Press, 2004), 216.

[40] Pierre Bourdieu, *Outline of a Theory of Practice* (Cambridge: Cambridge University Press, 2007), 167.

fathers of Folkish Asatru calls "the heroism and vitality of the Norsemen as depicted in popular literature."[41] This romanticized ideal of Viking life and culture has led to, as McNallen himself points out, a dynamic of communication and cooperation developing within Heathenry that is less than ideal. McNallen writes:

> It was a mistake to focus so strongly on the Norse experience ... instead of being Norse-centered, we would have done better to use the Germanic tribes as models ... the tribes demonstrate a better balance between the needs of the individual and the group, as well as a greater connection to kin and soil.[42]

While the past six years have seen a growing interest in Germanic tribes, within mainstream Asatru, the Norse model is still the dominant cultural model appropriated. It is significant that during the Viking Age so emulated by so much of modern American Asatru, the indigenous religion of northern Europe was already in its twilight.

2005-2006 were particularly formative years for Heathenry within the United States. The first public *blót* which included animal sacrifice was performed in 1995. With the founding of New Anglia Theod in 2004, such rituals became common and publicly discussed. The care and attention required in such a rite, particularly in caring for the animal, had the unexpected effect of causing many Heathens to give greater thought to the purpose of such rites. More than ever before in Heathenry, attention began to be directed not to lore, but to the Gods themselves.[43]

---

[41] Stephen McNallen, "Three Decades of Asatru Revival in America." in *Tyr: Myth, Culture, Tradition vol. 1 and 2,* ed. Joshua Buckley (Atlanta: Ultra Press, 2004), 205.

[42] Ibid., 216.

[43] S. Oberlander, personal communication with author, April 2, 2008.

At the same time, the Northern Tradition shamanic tradition, pioneered by non-Heathen Norse Pagan Raven Kaldera, became more organized and publicly active in ways that it had not been before. Several well-known Heathens became publicly affiliated with this movement. 2005 also saw the publication of the first devotional in contemporary Heathenry, this author's *Whisperings of Woden*[44]. This was followed by *Exploring the Northern Tradition*. In the four years since the publication of *Whisperings of Woden,* numerous devotionals have been published, nearly all of them coming from the Norse Pagan or Northern Tradition shamanic branches of the Northern Tradition.[45] A group of practitioners, under the aegis of Raven Kaldera, published a series of books on Northern Tradition shamanism detailing experiential techniques and focused predominantly on the *Jotnar* deities.[46] Additionally, a writer's collective was formed in 2006 to facilitate publication of these devotionals, which rarely appeal to large-scale publishers due to their limited market. Essentially, the mystics, shamans, and those involved in intense devotional practices came into the public eye like never before. They, and the doctrines they espoused, could no longer be ignored.

Northern-tradition shaman Raven Kaldera believes that the aggressive stance mainstream and orthodox Heathens take toward liminal practices and apparent deviations in orthodoxy stem in part from a desire of modern Heathens to avoid a "straw death" and thus to find their way into Valhalla. While the reasoning for this

---

[44] Galina Krasskova, *Whisperings of Woden: Nine Nights of Devotional Practice* (New York: BookSurge Publishing, 2004).

[45] Many (though not all) Norse Pagans and Northern Tradition shamans refuse to use the term "Heathen" for themselves due to the harassment they often receive within the mainstream Heathen community.

[46] The second major ideological fault line within Heathenry is whether or not the *Jotnar*, a family of deities associated with primal power, chaos, destruction, and initiation should be honored on par with the *Aesir*, deities of order and justice, and the *Vanir*, deities of fertility and abundance—or indeed honored at all.

may seem complex to one not versed in Heathen lore, he believes that modern Heathens popularly conflate Valhalla with the Christian heaven to some degree. Since the only way into Valhalla was to die a warrior's death in battle, and since our modern community no longer provides many opportunities for such a death on a large scale, modern Heathens have substituted aggressive, combative defense of "lore" and of their developing orthodoxy instead, in the unconscious belief that this symbolic battle will suffice to earn a place in this honored afterlife.[47]

This emphasis on orthodoxy as opposed to orthopraxy, combined with the need to publicly demonstrate worth through contest and struggle, has led to the dominant mode of communication throughout Heathenry being defined by its aggressive, seemingly inhospitable and occasionally hostile manner. In their article *The Pentagram and the Hammer*, considered seminal in Heathen circles, authors Lewis Stead and Devyn Gilette discuss this particular social trope:

> Ásatrúar tend to speak in a very direct method using declarative sentences, tending to cite things in a black and white and often simplistic manner. The general method of communication is to state one's position with the expectation that one's opposite will state theirs, and either agreement or argument will ensue. Consensus and compromise is rarely the object. This verbal sparring mirrors the general focus on conflict in the religion. A standoff between strong but disagreeing positions (i.e., agreeing to disagree) is generally seen as preferable to compromise. Face saving is seen to be the individual's own responsibility, to be obtained by demonstrating not only the validity of one's beliefs, but how strongly one holds them. Conversations

[47] Raven Kaldera, personal communication with author, November 10, 2007.

tend to be fast paced and often in emotional tones.
Any conflict and anger brought forth in debate is
generally dismissed as necessary to the process and
quickly forgotten; although when it is not, it tends
to create long-term grudges.[48]

Stead and Gilette rightly attribute this communication style to
a definitive reification of the past that so defines not only modern
Asatru, but modern Reconstructionist religions in general.[49] Like
Homeric Greek culture, Norse religionists draw their "personhood,
their social identity, from exchange, agonistic and otherwise." [50] It
may be that the hostility toward devotional practices and other
liminal practices may stem from a conflation of the receptivity
involved in devotional consciousness with weakness, unmanliness,
or submission. Certainly many of the public attacks against
Northern Tradition shamanism, deity-possession, and ecstatic
devotional practices condemn the apparent sacrifice of personal
agency and will involved.[51] According to Bourdieu:

> The structures constitutive of a particular type of
> environment ... produce *habitus,* systems of durable,
> transposable *dispositions*, structured structures
> predisposed to function as structuring structures...[52]

What Bourdieu calls *habitus* is the system of largely
unconscious structures that inform the development of attitudes,

---

[48] "The Pentagram and the Hammer" accessed November 10, 2007 from
<http://www.ravenkindred.com/wicatru.html>.

[49] At present, there are Reconstructionist Hellenic, Kemetic, Roman, Baltic,
Celtic, Norse, Sumerian, and Tribal Hebraic religions.

[50] T.O. Beidelman, "Agonistic Exchange: Homeric Reciprocity and the Heritage
of Simmel and Mauss." *Cultural Anthropology,* Vol. 4, No. 3 (August 1989), 6.

[51] S. Oberlander, personal communication with author, April 20, 2008.

[52] Pierre Bourdieu, *Outline of a Theory of Practice* (Cambridge: Cambridge
University Press, 2007), 72.

ideas, and ways of being in the world. It is the filter through which a particular people experience and translate their world. Within Heathenry, the dominant *habitus* has been created through a number of different but inter-related factors: the Protestant influence on modern Heathenry, the insistent reification of lore, hostility toward the more emotional aspects of spiritual expression, and the romanticization of late Viking-era culture. All of these things impact how the sacred is approached and what expectations the people involved have of those interactions. This is particularly apparent in the process of ritual.

There is very little formal ritual training offered within the Heathen community, even to those wishing to become clergy. While one national organization—the Troth—has attempted to create a clergy training program, the emphasis of this program (and others like it) lies predominantly in study of "lore". Religious rituals are primarily viewed as a means of building community. There is little understanding or desire in the majority of the community for rituals that create a palpable sense of the sacred external to that community building.[53] In fact, it seems likely that the reconstructed rituals of *blót* and *symbel* were primarily viewed at first as merely active extensions of the lore, a means of creating a community *Weltanschauung*. Certainly there is a marked ambivalence in Heathenry toward the Gods. In *Germanic Heathenry*, the only extant book on the modern reconstruction of Saxon-style Heathenry, author James Coulter writes about the process of *blót* (*bluostar* in Old High German, the Reconstructionist Saxon Heathen's liturgical language of choice):

> One should also know that point when it's simply 'too much of a good thing' – that is, yielding in excess or too frequently. ...If one offers overly frequently, it becomes more of an annoyance ... than a welcome

---

[53] Fuensanta Plaza, personal correspondence with author, April 25, 2008.

gift ... For every gift given, by either God or man, one is demanded ... in return."[54]

He goes on to speculate that making too many offerings (more than one or two a year) might offend the Gods, ostensibly because it is incomprehensible that one might give without expecting anything in return. Anglo-Saxon Heathen Swain Wodening describes *blót* as:

> Communion with one's Heathen friends and family, with one's ancestors, and the Gods. *Blót* is not so much a giving to the Gods as it is a way of sharing. It is a way of sharing food and drink in a way to create one big, happy community that includes the living and the dead. According to the Havamal, "a gift always expects a gift," in exchange for the food and drink we share with them, the ancestors and Gods ensure health and prosperity.[55]

The order in which Wodening lists the focal point of *blót* (community, ancestors and Gods) is not incidental. Greg Shetler in his popular book *Living Asatru,* says plainly that "ceremonies are social events."[56] He also notes, again quoting "a gift always expects a gift", that it is safer and better to "choose a gift up front, a sacrifice, and offer it in exchange for the help requested," rather than run the risk of the Gods actually demanding something of their own selection later.[57] The overwhelming majority of modern Heathens choose, therefore, to make not the sacred world of Gods and spirits the "axis around which the human world revolves,"[58]

---

[54] James Coulter, *Germanic Heathenry* (Texas: First Books Library, 2003), 154.

[55] Swain Wodening, *Hammer of the Gods* (Texas: Booksurge Press, 2003), 127.

[56] Greg Shetler, *Living Asatru* (Biloxi, MS: Imprint Books, 2005), 73.

[57] Ibid., 62.

[58] James Livingston, *Anatomy of the Sacred* (New Jersey: Pearson Prentice Hall, 2005), 46.

but rather choose instead to make the human world the axis around which the worlds of the Gods revolve, utilizing carefully structured public rituals to keep the sacred at bay. (The exception of course, is the Northern Tradition shamanic community, which focuses primarily on the Gods themselves.)

Additionally, the dominant bodily hexis, the "form of a pattern of postures that is both individual and systematic"—in other words the actual physical embodiment of culture—is largely informed by the prevailing distaste for emotional displays of devotion.[59] Indeed, this is one of the primary objections leveled against Northern Tradition shamans, mystics, and those seeking to establish an overarching "devotional consciousness": it is too body-centered, expressive, and messy.[60]

This is particularly apparent amongst those practicing Northern Tradition shamanism, in which body modification, bodily rituals that incorporate a certain degree of pain, and passionate expressions of religious ardor both verbally and in print, are the norm.[61]Part of the argument against such practices stems from the fact that the rare pain-based ordeal practices are generally adapted from the BDSM and body modification demographics, which in turn can be considered part of the "modern primitive" movement that has adapted ancient practices for the modern era.[62] Since contemporary Heathen ethics are largely informed by Protestantism (and within the United States, as noted previously, even the "unstated" religious assumptions of U.S. secularism are specifically Protestant), this also impacts ideas about the body, sexuality, and physical expression.

Saba Mahmood discusses the tension inherent in constructing a tradition, noting that the actual devotional and interpretive practices of the people can be markedly different from the arguments of textually-driven authorities. She points out that the

---

[59] Bourdieu, *Outline of a Theory of Practice*, 86.

[60] S. Oberlander, personal communication with author, April 5, 2008.

[61] Ibid.

[62] Raven Kaldera, personal communication with author, April 10, 2008.

tradition can be "constantly lived, reworked, and transformed in the context of daily interactions."[63] The field of discourse within Heathenry has been expanded from study and explication of lore-based exegesis to include bodily practice of ritual and personal interpretation of a doctrine already caught in its developmental flux. This has occurred largely through a growing number of adherents interested in exploring devotional practices and tangentially through the growing presence of the Northern Tradition shamanic community, which has been exceptionally prolific in publishing devotional material. It is, in its own way, becoming more "performatively constituted", albeit in ways that often create hostile and frenetic conflict with the dominant orthodoxies within the community.[64] Mahmood further elaborates on the interstices between tradition and active ritual practice:

> Tradition ... is not a set of symbols and idioms that justify present practices, neither is it an unchanging set of cultural prescriptions that stand in contrast to what is changing, contemporary, or modern. Nor is it a historically fixed social structure. Rather, the past is the very ground through which the subjectivity and self-understanding of a tradition's adherents are constituted.[65]

Ritual has also become the arena that some contemporary Heathens utilize to enforce specifically contested points of orthodoxy. Louisiana Heathen Whitney Braggisaga, who has been involved in Heathenry since 1982, comments on ritual as a means of preserving the community from contamination:

---

[63] Saba Mahmood, *Politics of Piety* (Princeton, NJ: Princeton University Press, 2005), 98.

[64] Ibid., 99.

[65] Ibid., 115.

We should *always* consider just who exactly it is that we are sharing a ritual horn with, not simply when we happen to be with one particular group or another. Just as we know to be careful about the oaths we swear, we should know to be vigilant about those with whom we blot.[66]

Part of this stems from the internal divisiveness between denominations over specific points of ideological debate, but part of it also stems, as Braggisaga goes on to note, from an understanding of theology drawn from personal practice:

I am sworn to Frigga. I serve as her handmaiden, her vassal, and her votary. I share her sorrow from the death of her son, and her determination to bring his murderers to justice, regardless of the cost. Her purpose of maintaining the home and family is my purpose as well.[67]

This type of assertion, based on personal gnosis (the idea of being sworn to a Goddess, as well as the idea that by worship one can cause a God's power to manifest) would have been unthinkable even a decade ago. Attitudes toward personal gnosis have slowly been evolving to accommodate some degree of experience. The past three years have also seen the idea of "PCPG" or "peer-corroborated personal gnosis" evolving from the Northern Tradition shamanic community and slowly making its way into the mainstream as a means of validating the personal experience.[68]

This modern body of religion is, as we have said elsewhere in this text, a work in progress and a work of constant change. The experience of the sacred through evolving ritual, and its effect its

---

[66] Whitney Braggisaga, personal correspondence with author, August 13, 2008.

[67] Ibid.

[68] Elizabeth Vongvisith, personal communication with author, April 10, 2008.

participants, is beginning to slowly alter the tradition of a religion created solely through reinterpretation of primary sources. It is this unspoken and often unacknowledged performativity that is contributing to the ongoing process of culture-building within the Northern Tradition, and it is the power of this performativity that may come to change the face of the modern Northern Tradition itself.

Bibliography

Beidelman, T.O. "Agonistic Exchange: Homeric Reciprocity and the Heritage of Simmel and Mauss," *Cultural Anthropology*, Vol. 4, No. 3 (August 1989). pp. 227-259.

Bourdieu, Pierre. *Outline of a Theory of Practice*. Cambridge: Cambridge University Press, 2007.

Campbell, Drew. "About Hellenismos," Ecauldron.com, 2005. <http://www.ecauldron.com/dc-faq.php>

Coulter, James. *Germanic Heathenry*. Texas: First Books Library, 2003.

Dubois, Thomas. *Nordic Religions in the Viking Age*. Philadelphia: University of Pennsylvania Press, 1999.

Durkheim, Emile. *The Elementary Forms of Religious Life*. Oxford: Oxford University Press, 2001.

Gardell, Mattias. *Gods of the Blood*. Philadelphia: University of Pennsylvania Press, 2003.

Jakobson, Janet and Pellegrini, Ann. *Love the Sin*. Boston: Beacon Press, 2004.

King, Richard. *Orientalism and Religion*. London: Routledge, 2005.

Krasskova, Galina. *Exploring the Northern Tradition*. New Jersey: New Page Books, 2005.

---. *Whisperings of Woden: Nine Nights of Devotional Practice*. New York: BookSurge Publishing, 2004.

Livingston, James. *Anatomy of the Sacred*. New Jersey: Pearson Prentice Hall, 2005.

McNallen, Stephen. "Three Decades of Asatru Revival in America." In *Tyr: Myth, Culture, Tradition vol. 1 and 2,* edited by Joshua Buckley. Atlanta: Ultra Press, 2004. pp. 203-220.

Magliocco, Sabina. *Witching Culture.* Philadelphia: University of Pennsylvania Press, 2004.

Mahmood, Saba. *Politics of Piety.* New Jersey: Princeton University Press, 2005.

Puryear, Mark. *The Nature of Asatru.* Nebraska: iUniverse, 2006.

Shetler, Greg. *Living Asatru.* Biloxi, Mississippi: Imprint Books, 2005.

Strmiska, Michael. "Ásatrú in Iceland: The Rebirth of Nordic Paganism?" *Nova Religio* 4, no. 1, 2000. pp. 106–132.

--- and Sigurvinsson, Baldur. "Asatru: Nordic Paganism in Iceland and America." In *Modern Paganism in World Cultures: Comparative Perspectives,* edited by Michael Strmiska. New York: ABC-CLIO, 2005. pp. 1-54.

Wodening, Swain. *Hammer of the Gods.* Texas: Booksurge Press, 2003.

Sacrifice, Odin, and the Ritual of *Blót* in Modern Heathenry

Over the past decade, the restoration of the ritual of sacrificial *blót* has become a mainstay of modern American Heathenry, Asatru and Northern Tradition Paganism.[1] This ritual, involving the structured sacrifice of an animal in a sacred setting, serves many different purposes within modern Heathenry, and has its origins in the twin motifs of conflict and violence inherent in Norse cosmology. This reconstructed ritual also highlights specific ideological differences between denominations and its evolving practice has also led to a greater emphasis on devotional work within this body of religions. This has raised both questions and controversy over the development of what this author terms "devotional consciousness" as well as highlighting the tension between textual authority and experiential power. The confluence of ideological tensions with the ideals of enlightenment through conflict so ingrained in Norse cosmology has directly influenced the manner in which sacrifice is approached, and its power as a ritual act within Norse Paganism flows directly from the dominant position of the high God Odin, a God not only of kingship but of violent personal sacrifice as well.

Asatru evolved simultaneously from several different ideological currents in America, Europe, and Iceland from 1968 to 1973.[2] The word itself comes from two Old Norse words: *Àsa* (Gods, possessive case) and *tru* (faith) or "faith in the Gods." The modern word is an Icelandic translation of a Danish word *Asetro*

---

[1] Hereafter referenced under the umbrella term "Heathenry".

[2] In Iceland, the religion drew heavily on environmentalist currents, in the US its earliest manifestations had connections to racialist and white identity movements. See Michael Strmiska, *Modern Paganism in World Cultures* (Santa Barbara: ABC-CLIO, 2005) and Jeffrey Kaplan, *Radical Religion in America* (Syracuse: Syracuse University Press, 1997).

which was first seen referenced in an article on Iceland in 1885.[3] Asatru is the main denomination of a body of religions collectively known by its practitioners as Heathenry.[4] It is polytheistic, focusing on the worship of exclusively Norse or Germanic Gods (i.e. Odin, Frigga, Freya, Thor, et al) ideally within a specific cultural context.[5] Since its formal founding in the early 1970's it has developed multiple denominations, a complex orthodoxy, ethical structure and extensive body of religious rites.[6] While most contemporary *blóts* involve only the sacrifice of large quantities of alcohol, the first formal *blót* involving animal sacrifice was performed in the United States in 1995.

This chapter will examine the ways in which sacrifice is approached within American Heathenry, particularly the manner in which the archetype of the sacrificial king has influenced the modern worship of Odin, one of the Norse Deities most often associated with sacrifice, and the ways in which that worship has influenced the *blót* setting.

Heathenry is best described as a body of religions that seek to reconstruct as accurately as possible the religious beliefs and to

---

[3] B. A. Robinson, "Asatru" *Religious Tolerance: World Religions,* <http://www.religioustolerance.org/asatru.htm>.

[4] "Heathenry" is an umbrella term encompassing the various Reconstructionist denominations of Norse Paganism, and Asatru is the most well-known, largest, and oldest of these denominations. In turn, both are under the larger umbrella term "Northern Tradition", which encompasses both Heathenry and the non-Reconstructionist Norse Pagan denominations. While the term Heathen is a pejorative to many outside this religious community, it has been adopted by this group of religions in much the same way that Wiccans have chosen to reclaim the word "witch".

[5] This reification of the past is a significant aspect of Reconstructionist Pagan religions—religions which seek to "reconstruct" practices of a specific culture as they existed prior to the insurgence of Christianity.

[6] This paper refers only to the American branches of this religion. Any further reference to Heathenry or Asatru within the body of this article, unless otherwise stated, refers only to American Asatru or Heathenry.

some degree social practices of pre-Christian polytheistic Northern Europe. All denominations share a common core cosmology, comparable ethics, and a unique body of what practitioners term "the lore": literary, scholarly, and historical texts that are studied by practitioners in order to provide a glimpse into the sacred stories, beliefs, and religious practices of pre-Christian Northern Europeans. While on the surface "the lore" is merely a collection of folklore, myths, modern historical analysis, and archaeological and anthropological writings, in practice it carries great normative authority within the religious community, giving commonly accepted interpretations the force of religious law.

Any examination of Heathenry is hampered by the paucity of both scholarly sources and the utter lack of archival materials from within the religion itself. Very little extant material exists focusing on tropes of sacrifice. For purposes of full disclosure, I myself am a practicing Northern Traditionalist and have been trained as *blótere*, or sacrificial priest. I have both observed and participated in numerous sacrifices over the past two decades. My position within this community has given me access to information and materials that an outsider might otherwise not be privy to. Conversely, my academic training hopefully has given me the tools to maintain the necessary distance and objectivity in discussing the dominant motifs related to sacrifice, myth, and ritual. Certainly as a religious studies scholar, the modern reconstruction of Norse Paganism presents a fascinating opportunity to watch the development of a religion through its earliest stages.

Heathenry and Sacrifice

While Heathenry has yet to be seriously explored by academics, there has been extensive study of the phenomenon of sacrifice within the world's religions, both ancient and modern. From Isaac to Iphigenia, the question of sacrifice has permeated both religious and academic thought. Certainly sacrifice has always been an integral part of worship and devotion within the Heathen religious traditions. As early as 98 CE, the Roman historian

Tacitus recorded the religious practices of the British Isles, noting that "Their holy places are woods and groves, and they apply the names of Deities to that hidden presence which is seen only by the eye of reverence."[7] He noted the practice of sacrifice amongst the Germanic tribes:

> Above all other gods they worship Mercury (Odin), and count it no sin, on certain feast-days, to include human victims in the sacrifices offered to him. Hercules (Thor) and Mars (Tyr) they appease by offerings of animals, in accordance with ordinary civilized custom.[8]

This is the earliest account known that specifically records the God Odin as having a particular penchant for human over animal sacrifice. Tacitus does not make any particular reference to other items being given in offering, but archaeological evidence supports the knowledge that weapons, jewelry, and assorted foodstuffs were also commonly offered. Clearly the practice of sacrifice in all its forms was of major ritual importance to the Germanic peoples of his time. Tacitus underscores the current of fear and dread underlying these sacrifices, noting their purpose of appeasement. He also equates the Norse Deities with comparable Roman ones; however, these attributions are not based on commonalities in sacrifice but rather on function. For instance, Odin—in addition to being a God of kings and warriors—is also a god of travel and poets, thus his association with Mercury. Mars was a God of war, as was Tyr, and both Hercules and Thor are known within their respective pantheons for their strength and protective natures.

Tacitus also offers the only surviving account of the worship of the Goddess Nerthus, whose rites at times may also have included human sacrifice:

---

[7] Cornelius Tacitus, *The Agricola and Germania*. Ed. James Rives, trans. by Harold Mattingly (London: Penguin Books, 2010), 109.

[8] Ibid., 108.

[T]hey share a common worship of Nerthus, or Mother Earth. They believe that she takes part in human affairs, riding in a chariot among her people. On an island of the sea stands an inviolate grove, in which, veiled with a cloth, is a chariot that none but the priest may touch. The priest can feel the presence of the goddess in this holy of holies, and attends her with deepest reverence as her chariot is drawn along by cows. Then follow days of rejoicing and merrymaking in every place that she condescends to visit and sojourn in. No one goes to war, no one takes up arms; every iron object is locked away. Then, and then only, are peace and quiet known and welcomed, until the goddess, when she has had enough of the society of men, is restored to her sacred precinct by the priest. After that, the chariot, the vestments, and (believe it if you will) the goddess herself, are cleansed in a secluded lake. This service is performed by slaves who are immediately afterwards drowned in the lake. Thus mystery begets terror and a pious reluctance to ask what that sight can be which is seen only by men doomed to die.[9]

Nerthus is representative of the cult of the Vanir, a family of fertility Gods worshipped in tandem with the Aesir, gods of order and justice. The God Freyr, also reverenced as both a God of sacrifice and kingship came from this family of Gods.[10] Despite earlier associations with sacrifice, by the late Viking age, Freyr was commonly considered to be a God of peace and fertility. Only Odin retained the unassailable association with sacrifice in general, and human sacrifice in particular within the cosmology.

---

[9] Tacitus, *The Agricola and Germania*, 135.

[10] E.O.G. Turville-Petre, *Myth and Religion of the North* (Connecticut: Greenwood Press, 1975), 173.

Frazer talks obliquely about this connection between fertility of the land and sacrifice embodied in rites like those described above, drawing a parallel between sacral kingship and the power of the sacred groves and forests inherent in the worship of specific Deities, particularly Diana and Virbius.[11] In many cases, the male consort of such Deities as Diana or Artemis, Cybele, or Selene represented the strength and fertility of the land and were, in their own time, sacrificed to ensure those blessings. In this way, the sacred figure of the king was a stand-in, or scapegoat for the land itself. The spilling of blood might be seen as analogous to the spilling of generative power (i.e. semen). In this way, Freyr is often represented in dominant iconography both ancient and modern by the erect phallus.

Given that the Germanic and Scandinavian tribes were primarily oral in nature, scholars and practicing Heathens alike are forced to rely on these first-hand accounts of travelers, tradesman and diplomats and on the writings of Christian historians and scribes for the majority of surviving material on religious customs and beliefs. The primary source of information comes from the Viking Age, 800 CE to 1300 CE. This was a time of extensive interaction through trade, migration and violent raiding. Viking trade routes spanned the continent of Europe extending throughout the North to what is now modern-day Russia, and even as far as the Ottoman Empire.[12] It was also a time when the religion was already in its decline due to the relentless spread of Christianity throughout Europe. This means that the majority of sources may or may not show extensive Christian influences. There is simply no way to know how corrupted the surviving material may be. Scholars must also contend with the question of

---

[11] James Frazer, *The Golden Bough*. (New York: The MacMillan Company, 1958), 9-10.

[12] K.C. Hulsman, *Heathen Magicoreligious Practices: From the Ancient Past Through the Reconstructed Present*. (Texas: University of Texas at Arlington, 2004), 1.1.

bias, as early Christians had no cause to accurately or fairly represent the beliefs of their Pagan forebears.

Regardless, there are numerous references to the practice of sacrifice in the Icelandic Sagas, and modern Heathen ritual style is based on this concept of giving libations to the Gods. In this context, sacrifice is best defined as an offering given to the Gods (or Goddesses), regardless of what is being offered. As such, sacrifice was seen as a means by which human beings could strengthen bonds of unity and kinship with the Gods.[13] This strengthening of the human-divine relationship was integral to the concept of *inangarð,* or the sacred enclosure of the community. Anything not encompassed within the boundaries of the community, not made licit by its incorporation into civilized, recognized society, was *utgarð,* or the outlands—unprotected, unhallowed, unsafe. One might see this concept of the sacred enclosure echoed in the often rigid taboos imposed on sacral kings. Frazer notes that monarchs in areas as far separated geographically as Tahiti, Mexico, and Japan were at one time forbidden to touch the ground outside of their own ancestral lands. Doing so consecrated the land, expanding the boundaries of what was sacred.[14] Taboo was used to ensure the inviolability of that which was decreed sacred. Within Heathenry, the rites of sacrifice were used in much the same way, by marking out the boundaries of what the Gods might licitly claim.

This idea of utilizing sacrifice to create bonds between Gods and man is quite old. Historian of religion Walter Burkert points out that "one of the clearest examples of Indo-European poetry that can be reconstructed from Greek and Sanskrit says that the

---

[13] In the "Rigsthula" (*Poetic Edda*), it is specifically stated that mankind is descended directly from the Gods. Scholars debate whether the God in question was Heimdallr (as most current Heathens believe) or Odin. There is a reference in the "Voluspa" that refers to mankind as "Heimdallr's children"; however, the *modus operandi* of the God disguised as Rig more closely fits that of Odin. Regardless, the outcome is the same: mankind is the direct progeny of the Gods.

[14] Frazer, *The Golden Bough,* 687.

gods are 'givers of good things,' *doteres eaon* in Homeric Greek."[15] He categorizes this type of sacrifice as one of *do ut des* or "I give so that you might give" and notes that it not only permeates ancient cultures but the Abrahamic religions as well.[16] It should come as no surprise that the same concept is found within Heathenry.

To the Heathen mind (both ancient and modern), sacrificial offerings were acts of *frith*[17] and hospitality. Nineteenth century scholar W. Grönbech defines *frith* as the embodiment of kinship and at the same time the conscious cultivation of sobriety, security, and balance.[18] It defines the boundaries of *inangarð*. In practice, it becomes not so much a means of resolving conflict as preventing or at the very least carefully ordering those conflicts that do arise. Yet there is something about the nature of *frith* that calls to mind the implacability of the Japanese *giri*: a word that means duty and the burden of obligation. In practice, this often involved wrenching sacrifice for the sake of upholding one's honor. The maintenance of *frith*, according to tales told in the surviving sagas, often carries with it a tragic element—suffering brought about by necessary action. In this way, ritual sacrifice might be seen as an act of *frith*; an act of extending necessary hospitality to the Gods thus ensuring greater sacrifices are not needed.

The importance of this hospitality to Heathen religious culture should not be underestimated, nor should its prevalence in the Eddas and Sagas. The modern Heathen community draws heavily on these medieval texts in formulating both the style of their rituals and the accepted approach to their Gods. The twinning of sacrifice with hospitality occurs early on in the

---

[15] Walter Burkert, *Homo Necans* (California: University of California Press, 1983), 135.

[16] Ibid., 136.

[17] Right order, often translated as "peace".

[18] Vilhelm Grönbech, *Culture of the Teutons, vol. 1* (Denmark: University of Cophenhagen, 1931), 58.

Eddas.[19] In the "Grimnismal", part of the *Poetic Edda*, the high God Odin gave blessings, wealth, fortune and rulership of a kingdom to a boy who had shown Him the very basic hospitality of offering Him a drink, while at the same time taking the life of the current king who had not. Hospitality was first and foremost a demonstration of one's character, and thought to bring the blessings of the Gods on one's house and line. Heathen author Swain Wodening notes:

> Hospitality was almost a necessity of survival for the ancient traveler. Weather could turn bad, there were no inns in that day, and a warm place to sleep was a welcome sight. Hospitality ensured the tribe's individuals would survive. One knew, that by putting up for the night, that someday the favor would be returned ... for the ancients this mutual cooperation meant mutual survival.[20]

Of course hospitality was not just a Northern European practice. Hospitality was equally important in Middle Eastern lands, ostensibly for much the same purpose. It was a means of protecting and binding the community together. In fact, so important a virtue was hospitality in the Middle Eastern world that in the Bible, Lot offers his home to two angels. When they are set upon by a mob of townspeople, he offers his own daughters

---

[19] The Poetic and Prose Eddas were written in the 13ᵗ century by poet and politician Snorri Sturluson. This places them two hundred years after the conversion of Iceland to Christianity, and several hundred years after the founding of Islam. While there is no clear way to know how much these traditions (particularly Christianity) influenced Sturluson's writing and interpretation of the surviving stories, the importance of hospitality is also attested to in earlier sources, including Tacitus's *Germania* in 98 C. E.

[20] Swain Wodening, *Hammer of the Gods* (Texas: Booksurge Press, 2003), 48.

(to be beaten, raped, and possibly killed) as a substitute rather than violate the tenets of hospitality toward his guests.[21]

Today, hospitality is one of the "Nine Noble Virtues", ethical mores held sacred by many modern-day Heathens.[22] It is one of the few values that the differing denominations of Heathenry agree upon. In fact, the entire concept of *frith* or right action within one's community is based in large part on hospitality. This is not surprising. Since large sacrifices were often held as part of a communal feast, by extension they also helped to strengthen the bonds of community.[23] Furthermore, within Norse culture, gift-giving had specific connotations of reciprocal obligation.

---

[21] Genesis 19:8.

[22] The Nine Noble Virtues are courage, discipline, industriousness, hospitality, self-reliance, perseverance, truth, honor and fidelity. These nine virtues have been drawn by modern practitioners from the stories in the *Poetic Edda*. Self-reliance in particular is emphasized, often to the perceived detriment of the community. Very little attention is given to mercy, compassion, or piety, despite the fact that the latter virtue at least was of grave importance in other Paganisms of the time. Modern Heathens dismiss such virtues as products of Christianization, preferring to cling to a romanticization of the ideals of late Viking age warrior culture.

[23] This was not the case in all ancient cultures. Ancient Hebrew culture for instance, forbade the consumption of the sacrificial meal out of an awareness of the animal's sanctity. (Smith, p. 346). No such attitude permeated Heathen consciousness, though in some cases, as with ancient Roman sacrifices, part of the animal might be reserved for the Gods, and part shared with the people. In modern cases where the entire animal is offered in immolation, the reason is ascribed to the God's (usually Odin's) greedy hunger rather than any inherent holiness of the animal itself. It is not the animal that is viewed as inviolable but the act and ritual of sacrifice itself. Fire does not seem to have been a means of offering sacrifice prior to the modern restoration of Heathenry. This likely stems from the fact that the Gods of fire in Norse cosmology were viewed as largely inimical to Godly order and to humanity. Creation begins not with the utterance of Divine will as in Judaic scripture, nor with an act of singular ejaculation as with some version of ancient Egyptian creation mythos, but with a violent conflict of opposites: the world of ice and fire collided and from this a hermaphroditic proto-being was born. Creation happened around the sleeping body of this being and eventually three Gods rose up (Odin being one of them), slaughtering this primal giant and creating the human world from his bones.

There are no free gifts, especially within Heathenry. Even within the modern community the giving of a gift in a ritual setting is one of the accepted ways of establishing and demonstrating hierarchy and social dominance. Essentially, the act of giving a gift required some form of payment in return, which in and of itself committed the giver and receiver to an endless cycle of reciprocity.[24] The giving and receiving of a gift was a terrifying and dangerous thing, fraught not only with social obligations but with spiritual ones as well. This is best illustrated in the *Havamal* where the God Odin states: *Betra er óbeðit en sé ofblótit, ey sér til gildis gjöf; betra er ósent en sé ofsóit.* ('Tis better not to pray than too much offer; a gift ever looks to a return. 'Tis better not to send than too much consume.)[25]

This concept of reciprocity is particularly important in light of how modern Heathens approach sacrificial rituals. Giving a gift requires that something be given in return. This creates in the mind of the giver an inviolable bond.[26] The entire cycle is based on constraint, hence modern Heathens who practice animal sacrifice approach the ritual with marked ambivalence. One Heathen priest, Jeffrey Runokivi, a participant in the first *blót* performed in the United States in 1995, went so far as to say that "in *blót* there is no room for joy."[27] This seems a startling statement, and in many modern Heathens, this ambivalence

---

The Gods of fire, according to the myth of Ragnarok, return at the end of time to destroy the Gods of order and with them the human world. The only use of fire attested to in the Icelandic sagas involves carrying torches around a sacred site to hallow it. This practice is done today. The use of fire to immolate offerings is solely a modern practice. I believe it is born largely out of expediency, but it could just as easily be an outgrowth of the Judeo-Christian consciousness with which the majority of modern Heathens were raised.

[24] Marcel Mauss, *The Gift* (NY: W. W. Norton, 1990), ix.

[25] Seagmund Sigfusson, "Havamal" in *Poetic Edda,* trans. Benjamin Thorpe, The Erickson Family Web Site.
<http://www.glenreva.com/history/lineTwo/elderEddaOdin.htm>.

[26] Mauss. *The Gift,* 13.

[27] Jeffrey Runokivi, personal correspondence with author, March 16, 2006.

toward sacred power goes beyond distaste into outright denial of even the possibility of direct experience.

Sociologist Emile Durkheim, in his pioneering work *The Elementary Forms of Religious Life,* points out that the sacred world and the mundane world are always separate, by their very definitions of each other. Moreover, that which is sacred is invested with a quality of contagion, allowing it to infiltrate the world of the profane unless carefully bounded by taboo and necessary precautions.[28] Any breech of these carefully defined territories may cause fear, ambivalence, and hostility. Within modern Heathenry, all rituals—but particularly those involving sacrifice—are approached with a tension approaching outright fear of exactly that: fear that the world of the profane will be contaminated by that which is sacred. Runokivi speaks of being filled with "holy terror" at the thought of what might have happened if he had failed to perform the *blót* successfully. Gerd Axenthowes, who, along with Jeffrey Runokivi and Garman Lord, performed the first formal public *blót* in modern Heathenry, notes:

> A *blót* tends to be a test of the man *blóting* and those around him. There is, though, to my mind some problem with seeing a *blot* simply as an offering. A *blót* involves taking something rather mundane (a meat animal) and making it holy, then in the act of eating it, as well as the act of asperging, the folk share in the holiness of the gods. It is not simply giving an offering, it is bringing gods and men closer to each other through the mediation of the *blót* beast.[29]

This Old Norse word for ritual sacrifice, *blót,* is used by the majority of modern Heathens to indicate a ritual in which

---

[28] Emile Durkheim, *Elementary Forms of Religious Life* (Oxford: Oxford University Press, 2001), 236-237.

[29] Runokivi, personal communication with author, March 16, 2006.

offerings are given to the Gods, often some type of blood sacrifice.[30] It was originally thought to translate as "to strengthen" (the Gods).[31] Given the reciprocal obligations of gift-giving among the Norse, it would follow that strengthening the Gods led to a strengthening of one's personal health, wealth, luck and well-being as well as that of one's kin.

"Animal sacrifice was an all-pervasive reality in the ancient world" and the association of holy rituals with bloodshed is also an ancient one.[32] Burkert goes so far as to theorize that "sacrificial killing is the basic experience of the sacred".[33] At the same time, historian Miranda Green notes that "sacrificial ceremonies were ... associated with rejoicing, with festivities and thanksgiving; they were perceived to facilitate communication with the divine world and therefore to be a cause for elation."[34] What both authors agree on is that sacrifice involving some form of bloodshed was ubiquitous throughout the ancient world. The idea of making something *sacer*, i.e. holy, often involved sending it to the God directly![35] Indeed, the sacrifice itself was but a means to an end. It was not the end in and of itself. It was performed to bring specific benefits to individuals and/or communities.[36]

Historically, the Germanic and Scandinavian peoples offered a plethora of items in sacrifice, not just animals, and by and large this holds true for the modern Heathen community today as well. Only a very small percentage of modern Heathens have performed or even witnessed a traditional *blót* (i.e. one in which an animal is sacrificed) despite the fact that the idea of *blót*

---

[30] *Blót* is pronounced to rhyme with "boat".

[31] Rudolf Simek, *Dictionary of Northern Mythology* (Suffolk, UK: St. Edmundsbury Press, 1993), 271.

[32] Burkert, *Homo Necans,* 9.

[33] Ibid.

[34] Miranda Green, *Dying for the Gods* (UK: Tempus Books, 2002), 19.

[35] Not surprising, really, given that the word *sacer* also means "belonging to the Gods".

[36] Green, *Dying for the Gods,* 20.

is becoming extremely powerful within the community consciousness. Perhaps because there are clear accounts in the surviving sources attesting to its importance in pre-Christian religious culture, *blót* holds a privileged place in the modern Heathen psyche. In fact, the most common sacrificial item is alcohol. Among the ancient Germanic tribes, historian Miranda Green notes that:

> [W]eapons—particularly swords and spears— were habitually snapped or savagely bent out of shape, presumably as an act of sacred destruction. Aggression appears to have been a significant component in certain rites of offering to, or communicating with, the gods.[37]

The destruction, in some way, of items destined for sacrifice is seen by both modern practitioners and scholars as a means of rendering those items unfit for human use. Just as the sacrifice of a human being through killing removed that human from the temporal world, so breaking or otherwise disfiguring offerings served the same purpose. The aggressive element inherent in this destruction is seldom discussed, yet it seems that it serves precisely the same purpose as killing; it removes the object being sacrificed from human use. The only difference lies in how one chooses to privilege that which is being sacrificed.

Additionally, Green references René Girard, who developed the idea of mimetic desire and of sacrifice as a form of scape-goating designed to maintain cohesion and stability within a given community. In *Violence and the Sacred* he notes:

> All religious rituals spring from the surrogate victim, and all the great institutions of mankind, both secular and religious, spring from ritual ... It could

---

[37] Ibid., 50.

hardly be otherwise, for the working basis of human thought, the process of 'symbolization,' is rooted in the surrogate victim.[38]

He proposed that sacrifice was an ambivalent practice, one that was both beneficial and harmful at the same time. He also connects all sacrifice back to primal rivalries, to an act of violence that calms growing rivalries and tensions within a specific social group. For Girard, the symbolic repetition of this scape-goating underlies all acts of religious violence.

While this may hold true in many religious traditions, it does not seem to be the dominant trope within Heathenry. The ambivalence that modern Heathens evince toward the act of sacrifice (and toward ritual in general) has more to do with a certain ambivalence toward the concept of Deity inherent in the modern Reconstruction, growing as it does out of a post–Enlightenment and post-Modern culture, than it does with any violence inherent in the process of sacrifice itself. Girard's theory seems to privilege violence in a way that discounts the impact the direct experience of the numinous can have upon a person or a community. The surviving sources relating to pre-Christian Norse Paganism indicate that it was this experience underlying the ritual process that led to the sacrifice of various items, up to and including animals and people. Sacrifice stemmed from the understanding of hospitality one might show an honored guest, with the provision of food as the most essential form of nourishment. It was also tied in to the medium of exchange. The reasons for nourishing the Gods may have come from a sense of fear over the power of the Gods to bring both luck and disaster, but ritual scape-goating was not part of that process. That being said, the shedding of blood did hold a unique power over the

---

[38] Rene Girard, *Violence and the Sacred* (Baltimore: John Hopkins University Press, 1977), 306.

Heathen religious mind, and to some degree continues to do so today.[39]

While the nature of the sacrifice depended largely upon the nature of the Deity in question, the confluence of violence and flesh sacrifice forms a fundamental trope within Northern Cosmology, one that is essential in providing necessary understanding of the ideals of conflict and sacred power that form the ideological basis of the modern body of Reconstructed religions.[40] As shall be shown below, this trope revolved around one of the most well-known Gods in the Northern pantheon, a God commonly associated not only with sacrifice but also with kingship and magic: Odin.

Sacrifice and Norse Cosmology

The attitudes of Heathens on the subject of sacrifice are many and varied. Then as now, certain types of sacrifices were (and are) very strongly associated with certain Deities. For instance, it is known that in the Viking era, human sacrifice was occasionally performed, as within most cultures at some point or another throughout history. (It goes without saying that human sacrifice

---

[39] I qualify this because the impact of the Enlightenment and Post-Modernism on contemporary approach to religion in general and Gods in particular cannot be under-estimated. The majority of modern Heathens come from a fundamentalist Protestant upbringing, and these two factors more than any other have had tremendous impact on ritual work within the tradition. There is almost a sense of embarrassment over the emotions ritual has the power to evoke and modern rituals have been structured to limit any direct experience with the numinous.

[40] *Reconstructionist* is a term that has come into common usage over the past decade within contemporary Paganisms to define those religions, like Asatru or Heathenry, which adhere strictly to one cosmology, draw heavily on one specific culture—in this case Norse or Germanic—and look to a specific body of texts to guide the development of their religion. In addition to Heathenry and/or Asatru, there is are also Celtic, Kemetic, Baltic (called Romuva), Greek (called Hellenismos), Roman, Sumerian and Canaanite Reconstructed Paganisms.

plays no part in modern Heathen rituals.)[41] One common means of human sacrifice in the Norse world involved hanging the victim while at the same time stabbing him with a spear. This was the traditional means of sacrificing a man to Odin, because Odin hung on the Tree of Wisdom to acquire knowledge, pierced with His own spear.

Odin is the high God in the Northern tradition. He has many by-names[42] and is generally referred to both in the surviving sources and in modern Heathenry as the All-Father, Victory Father, Hanging God, Old Man, or Old One-Eye. One of the defining aspects of His nature, as attested to in the Norse myths, was His insatiable thirst for knowledge and wisdom. Modern Northern Tradition shamans like Raven Kaldera refer to Odin as the "God of the Ordeal." The Ordeal Path, as practiced by modern Northern Tradition shamans (and others), involves the "intentional and careful use of pain in order to put the body into an altered state."[43] One could say that the use of pain in such a fashion lies at the heart of Odin's sacrifice.[44]

The story of Odin's primary ordeal is told in the *Havamal*, one of the lays of the *Poetic Edda*. The reader is told that in search of wisdom, Odin hung himself for nine days and nights on Yggdrasil, the World Tree. While Odin is usually viewed as a God of kingship, he also holds a place within the Northern Tradition as a God of shamans. The idea of a great cosmic tree which

---

[41] The exception to this might be found in the Northern Tradition shamanic community where a growing number of devotees name themselves *godatheow* ("god-slaves"), or *living* sacrifices to a specific Deity.

[42] Odin has over 100 by-names or *heiti* listed in the surviving lore.

[43] Raven Kaldera, "The Eightfold Path to Altered States of Consciousness" Northern Tradition Shamanism,
<http://www.northernshamanism.org/shamanic-techniques/eight.html>

[44] So much so that one modern ordeal worker, Anya Kless, a devotee of Odin, refers to Him by the names "Thirsty for Pain" and "Hungry for Flesh". She is not alone in these attributions within the Northern Tradition community. Similar comments can frequently be heard, made by devotees of Odin— particularly those who also identify as ordeal workers.

supports the universe and which can be utilized by shamans in spirit-travel is common to many northern European cultures, most notably the Yakut and Buryat.[45] The Tree shows up again in Jewish Kabbalah in the guise of the Tree of Life, and has its earliest manifestation in Sumerian stories of the Goddess Inanna. It is by traversing the World Tree that Odin is able to move from his role as sacred king to that of shaman. The key to this transition from temporal to liminal power was his sacrifice via hanging.

During this ordeal, he starved and stabbed himself with his own spear, shedding his own blood. Eventually he died. It is through his death and rebirth that gained access to the runes, keys to the secrets of the universe:

> I ween that I hung on the windy tree,
> Hung there for nights full nine;
> With the spear I was wounded, and offered I was
> To Othin, myself to myself,
> On the tree that none may ever know
> What root beneath it runs.[46]

Odin then recites the charms that he learned and lays down the formula for making appropriate sacrifices by providing a list of ritual acts including divination, blood offering, petitioning the Gods and making actual sacrifice.[47] While many modern Heathens look at this passage as esoteric lore solely concerned with the reading of runes for divination, many scholars most notably German historian Rudolf Simek believe it to be a complex list of ritual actions, one that specifically references sacrifice.[48] Odin's

---

[45] Mircea Eliade, *Shamanism: Archaic Techniques of Ecstasy* (Princeton: Princeton University Press, 1964), 69-70.

[46] Henry Bellows, *The Poetic Edda* (New York: The American Scandinavian Foundation, 1926), 60.

[47] Simek, *Dictionary of Northern Mythology*, 272. See also *Havamal* stanza 144.

[48] Ibid.

sacrifice permeates modern Heathen consciousness. It is one of the defining moments in the religion's mythos.

The use of pain as a spiritual tool is quite controversial in modern Heathenry, perhaps even more so than the idea of animal sacrifice itself. It is however, part and parcel of Odin's story. In his book *Dark Moon Rising*, Kaldera notes that "cultures all over the world have explored ways to use the power of pain as a spiritual tool."[49] He makes reference to the Lakota Sun Dance, the Hindu Kavadi and notes that "the technique of applied pain is probably older than that of psychoactive substances," yet another shamanic practice that Odin is associated with.[50] While Northern Tradition shamanic practices are somewhat outside the scope of this paper, the idea of sacrifice and/or pain to gain wisdom is deeply entrenched in the core cosmological ethos of northern religions. This has evolved within a subsection of modern Heathenry into the practice of "ordeal work".

Ordeal work is a fairly modern subculture term that came into use in the early 1990s by people who came out of the BDSM, body modification, and "hook-sports" (i.e. recreational flesh suspension) demographics, and who wanted a term with an emphasis on the psychological and spiritual rather than on the recreational. Ordeal work refers to a body of practices used to inflict a deep catharsis on an individual for purposes such as self-growth, religious sacrifice, or rites of passage. These practices most often involve physical pain or endurance. It is usually done in a spiritual or at least a carefully crafted context. Regardless of the religion involved, the lexicon of pain remains the same; according to ordeal workers, the viscera of these practices, when utilized in a controlled manner have the power to heal, transform, and render the practitioner receptive to their Gods.

---

[49] Raven Kaldera, *Dark Moon Rising: Pagan BDSM and the Ordeal Path* (MA: Asphodel Books, 2006), 39.

[50] Ibid.

The physical techniques utilized in ordeal are varied, but often include (either singly or in various combinations) scalpel cuttings that are rubbed with hot ash, branding with a cautery pen, skin removal (a type of controlled flaying), tattooing (usually after the ordeal itself), hook suspension, hook pulls, flogging, having needles inserted through the skin in specific patterns, sensory deprivation, endurance rituals, and ritual psycho-drama. All of these practices have their corollaries in the ancient world. Priests of the Goddess Cybele, for example, would slash their bodies with knives, giving their own blood in offering. At its most extreme manifestation, devotees would castrate themselves in a similar manner at the conclusion of rituals filled with ecstatic dancing.[51] During specific religious festivals, Hindu devotees may perform *Kavadi*: piercing the body with hooks or spikes, ideally to provoke spirit possession.[52]

Lest this be mistaken for an Eastern phenomenon, it is worth noting that Native Americans, across tribal denominations, still perform the Sun Dance, a sacrificial dance in which dancers have hooks inserted into their flesh, which are then secured to a central tree or post (again, we see the imagery of the tree recurring as a central theme). They then dance until the hooks tear free of their flesh.[53] We also have the example of Christian *flagellantes*, who still perform rites of flagellation in honor of Christ in contemporary Spain. By engaging in such practices, practitioners of the ordeal position themselves as living sacrifices to their Gods. It is not coincidental that the majority of ordeal workers within the Northern Tradition are devotees of Odin. Historian E. Turville-Petre points out that

[T]he sacrifice of Odin to himself may ...be seen as the highest conceivable form of sacrifice, in fact so

---

[51] Frazer, *The Golden Bough*, 405.

[52] Ariel Glucklich, *Sacred Pain* (UK: Oxford University Press, 2001), 115.

[53] Ibid., 144-47.

high that, like many a religious mystery, it surpasses our comprehension. It is the sacrifice, not of king to god, but of god to god of such a kind as is related in Scripture of the sacrifice of Christ.[54]

Nor was this similarity with the sacrifice of Christ lost on early converts to Christianity. One of the earliest known Anglo-Saxon Christian poems, dating from the 7th century C.E., *The Dream of the Rood,* uses imagery suited to both Christ and Odin and Pagan themes abound:

> *The young hero stripped himself—he, God Almighty—strong and stout-minded. He mounted high gallows, bold before many, when he would loose mankind. I shook when that Man clasped me. I dared, still, not bow to earth, fall to earth's fields, but had to stand fast. Rood was I reared. I lifted a mighty King, Lord of the heavens, dared not to bend. With dark nails they drove me through: on me those sores are seen, open malice-wounds. I dared not scathe anyone. They mocked us both, we two together. All wet with blood I was, poured out from that Man's side, after ghost he gave up. Much have I born on that hill of fierce fate. I saw the God of hosts harshly stretched out.[55]*

Here the reader is presented with the image of a warrior-Christ, courageously sacrificing himself. The poem is told from the perspective of the tree itself, and the reference to the tree as a gallows willingly mounted would immediately conjure the image of Odin to the Pagan mind. One of his by–names was, after all, "the Gallows God" (Yggdrasil being viewed as a type of gallows).

---

[54] Turville-Petre, *Myth and Religion of the North,* 48.

[55] *The Dream of the Rood,* accessed March 22 from <http://faculty.uca.edu/jona/texts/rood.htm>.

Christ, like Odin, is also viewed as a mighty king, and both shared the attribution of "lord of hosts".

In short, both Odin and Christ hung and died. Both were pierced by a spear. Both rose again into new life. Both were seen as sacral kings. The difference between them lies in the reasons behind their respective sacrifices: Christ, according to common Christian interpretation, hung to free mankind of their sins—in other words as a scapegoat; Odin hung for himself alone, to deepen his wisdom and expand his power to order the world at large. He hung to gain sovereignty as a king, not just over the temporal world but over the spirit world as well. The only way to gain and master the wisdom of the dead was to die. Frazer points out that kings were often revered not merely as rulers but also as priests, intercessors between the human world and the gods. This in part stemmed from the ritual deification of the king as a divine figure himself.[56] In Odin, the function of king is united with the function not only of priest but also of magician and shaman. That union occurs through consciously sought out ordeals, and each ordeal involves some form of sacrifice.

Hanging on Yggdrasil was not the only sacrifice that Odin made in the surviving mythos. In addition to his sacrifice on the World Tree, He also hung suspended between two fires in the *Grimnismal* and plucked out an eye in payment for a single drink from the Well of Memory and Wisdom. This willing loss of an eye is particularly interesting. Odin is never depicted in any known image or account with both eyes intact. This loss of one eye, and the resulting iconography of this God as one-eyed, is one of his defining symbols within Norse cosmology. Unlike the blind seer Tiresias of Greek mythos, Odin was not blinded as a result of experienced wisdom, or by a punitive Deity; rather, he chose consciously to partially blind himself in order to gain wisdom. His blinding was then, an act of power.

---

[56] Frazer, *The Golden Bough,* 11.

The submission to pain as an act of personal empowerment raises many questions not only about the nature of pain but also about the nature of personal agency. A clear distinction must be drawn between "pain as a *cause* of action," and "pain as a *kind* of action."[57] It is this latter manifestation of pain encompassed by Odin's story. Here, pain is used not as an externally repressive measure, but as an expression of personal sovereignty. [58] Anthropologist Talal Asad notes that "when we say that someone is suffering, we commonly suppose that he or she is not an agent. To suffer ... is, so we usually think, to be in a passive state—to be an object, not a subject."[59] In Odin, however, the reader is presented with the image of a suffering body engaged in an act of power, or, as modern ordeal workers might phrase it, "hunting for power".[60] In such a context, pain loses its emotional charge and becomes a consciously applied tool in a greater process of development. Pain becomes something more than a private experience, or an experience of utter loss of control. It becomes an act of power, one that sets the defining tone for an entire religious tradition.

Not only pain, but blindness and the paradox of sacrificing sight in order to gain vision, permeates Odin's mythos. Several of his *heiti* or by-names refer to his vision: *Blindr*: blind one, *Gestumblindi*: the blind guest; *Tviblindi*: doubly blind. According to Indo-European historian Kris Kershaw, by looking at the context in which this name is used in the poetic sources, this intriguing by-name designates Odin not only as one who is himself blind, but also as one who has the power to strike others blind (be it as a battle tactic, or perhaps blind with ecstasy or

---

[57] Talal Asad, *Formations of the Secular* (California: Stanford University Press, 2003), 69.

[58] Ibid., 71.

[59] Ibid.,79.

[60] Krasskova, currently unpublished article "Ordeal Work, Body Modification, and the Use of Pain in Modern Norse Paganism." First presented October 4, 2008 at a religious studies conference at Ohio State University.

desire, two qualities also associated strongly with this God).[61] We also have *Gunnblindi*: he who strikes others blind in battle, *Herblindi*: he who strikes armies with blindness, and *Bileygr*: weak-eyed as well as *Bálegyr*: flaming eye.[62] Given the cliché in English of the eyes as windows to the soul, one might infer that in sacrificing one eye, Odin sacrificed part of his soul in exchange for wisdom, hearkening back to the Eddic proverb that a gift demands equal gift.

Odin is one of several mutilated or self-mutilating Gods in Northern European mythology. In Irish mythology, for instance, King Nuada of the Tuatha de Danaan lost an arm in battle and later replaced it with a functioning silver replica. In Norse Mythology, the God Tyr sacrifices a hand. There is also another blind God—Hodr—amongst the Norse pantheon but almost nothing has survived about his function. While the particulars of Hodr's blindness are unknown, in the cases of both Nuada and Tyr, their respective sacrifices occurred as a necessary exchange for the protection and security of their people: Nuada lost his arm in battle ending a great war that was destroying his people, and Tyr sacrificed his hand to Fenris, the wolf of chaos and destruction, in order to bind the animal and thus prevent it from its fated goal of bringing destruction to the Gods. It is a small step from the idea of physical mutilation as sacrifice to the idea of human sacrifice.

As noted earlier, Tacitus makes note of human sacrifice to Odin in *Germania,* and apparently this was done in a very specific manner: usually by hanging the victim while piercing his side with a spear. One of the most well-known examples of a sacrifice of this kind to Odin occurs in Gautrek's Saga, a 13th century retelling of the story of Odinic hero Starkadr. It includes a tale of sacrifice

---

[61] Kris Kershaw, *The One Eyed God* (Washington, D.C.: Journal of Indo-European Studies Monograph Number Thirty-Six, 2000), 3.

[62] Kershaw notes that this specifically indicates that Odin has the power to blind armies with terror during battle. But given that Odin is traditionally known as a God of warriors, it seems to me that it could just as easily be translated as one who blinds his armies *to* terror.

centering on Starkadr's King, Vikarr. While sailing, King Vikarr
and his crew (which included his friend, blood brother and one of
Odin's chosen heroes: the aforementioned Starkadr) experienced
horrible storm winds. They cast runes to determine how to calm
the storm and as the storm winds abated, it was revealed through
divination that Odin demanded a sacrifice. Turville-Petre notes
that Odin was usually placated by *royal* victims, perhaps a nod to
his role as sacred king.[63] The majority of recorded victims in the
surviving skaldic narratives were kings or princes, usually warriors.
The men drew lots to determine who should be sacrificed and
predictably it turned out to be the king himself. (By drawing lots,
the choice was automatically put into the hands of Odin and the
Fates.) Therefore the men decided to hold a symbolic sacrifice
rather than actually killing their King. The men fastened a cord
made of calf gut loosely around Vikarr's neck tying the other end
to a thin branch. Neither would bear a man's weight. Starkadr
then struck the King with a slender reed uttering the words "Now
I give thee to Odin." At that moment, the reed became a spear
and the cord a rope noose and the King was sacrificed for true.[64]

The sacrifice of a king is well known throughout folklore.
Frazer notes that kings were often sacrificed as old age or infirmity
took hold. In other cases, the king might be sacrificed at the end
of a fixed period of time. There is a story, for instance, linking
Odin with this latter type of sacrifice. Frazer writes of King Aun of
Sweden who sacrificed extensively of Odin and received the gift
that he would be allowed to live and reign for however long he
continued to sacrifice one of his sons every nine years. This
continued for nine consecutive sacrifices until the king was so
feeble (and ostensibly incompetent) that his own people prevented
the tenth sacrifice.[65] There is no indication in the story of Vikarr

---

[63] Turville-Petre, *Myth and Religion of the North,* 47.

[64] "King Gautrek's Saga" in *Seven Viking Romances,* trans. Magnus *Magnusson and
Hermann Palsson* (Penguin Books, 1980), 71. My paraphrase.

[65] Frazer, *The Golden Bough,* 324.

that the king was anything less than capable. Rather it seems that Odin, as God of warriors, might instead choose the best and most virile of kings to join him in Valhalla, the hall to which the valorous were believed to go after death. The offering of Vikarr brings to the fore not only Odin's connection to kings and warriors, but also his role as sacrificial God. Starkadr becomes the sacrificial priest as Odin had earlier predicted (in the story, Starkadr is warned that he is fated by Odin to commit three horrible deeds, of which the killing of Vikarr is one).

Of course, Starkadr's intent was to trick the God by offering a mock-sacrifice, almost a substitution, in which no blood was spilt. One might say that at that very moment, Vikarr became *homo sacer,* inviolable sacrifice (perhaps by virtue of his sacred stature, the king being at once the embodiment of the law and outside of the law).[66] Hence in the story, it was the will of the God manifesting through the unwitting Starkadr, by which the king was killed. This in and of itself was a cross-contamination of sacred act/time/space with the profane. Ironically as the men attempted to make one substitution, Odin effectively "turned the tables" and made his own.

Blót in the modern community

By the late Viking age, human sacrifice was no longer part of the prevailing ritual practice. Animal sacrifice, however, continued to be practiced extensively, and until the closing of the last Heathen temple in Upsalla in 1100 CE it was common to sacrifice a boar on Yule to ensure a good harvest, the boar being associated with abundance and luck in Norse cosmology.

These ritual sacrifices followed a set structure. Prior to the sacrifice, the animal was led around the hall and people would take holy oaths by laying their hands on the animal's back.[67] There is

---

[66] Giorgio Agamben, *Homo Sacer* (California: Stanford University Press, 1998), 15, 72-73.

[67] Simek, *Dictionary of Northern Mythology,* 298.

some evidence that—as with ancient Roman sacrifices—divination was performed after the animal was killed.[68] The only recorded instances in Scandinavian lore in which the animal was not eaten occur either when one was requesting a direct favor from the Gods or in the practice of *seidhr* magic.[69] Interestingly enough, this same pattern may be found in some modern Afro-Caribbean religions in which animal sacrifice is an essential part: an animal sacrifice in exchange for a specific boon or to work some type of charm is never consumed.[70]

The format of standard rituals within modern Heathenry is largely drawn from descriptions such as the one from the Icelandic Sagas (described in the last essay on p. 26-27 of this book), and other first- and second-hand sources of the time: The folk gather and the space is hallowed. The Gods and/or Goddesses are invoked and all the offerings are blessed. A horn of alcohol, usually mead, is passed around and each person individually hails

---

[68] This is referenced particularly in the Ynglinga Saga. Snorri Sturluson, "Yngling Saga" in *Heimskringla*, trans. Lee M. Hollander (University of Texas Press, 1991).

[69] *Seidhr* is perhaps best described as a form of Northern sorcery, though modern Heathens occasionally misuse the term to refer to a type of oracular divination. It did not need to include blood offerings, however there is a reference in Kormak's Saga to a *seidhrkona* (*seidhr* practitioners were almost always female, as there was a certain taboo against male *seidhr*-workers in old Norse culture) who sacrifices geese in order to perform magic.

> *The third time, just as Kormak came out, she had killed two geese and let the blood run into a bowl, and she had taken up the third goose to kill it. "What means this business, foster-mother?" said he. "True it will prove, Kormak, that you are a hard one to help," said she. "I was going to break the spell Thorveig laid on thee and Steingerd. Ye could have loved one another and been happy if I had killed the third goose and no one seen it."*

Kormak's Saga, trans. W.G. Collingwood and J. Stefansson, Online Medieval & Classical Library, <http://sunsite.berkeley.edu/OMACL/Cormac/>

[70] K. Foisy, personal communication with author, March 26, 2009. Taken from a discussion about the uses of ritual sacrifice.

the Deities in question. Depending on the nature of the ritual, the horn may be passed three times. If the rite includes animal sacrifice, it occurs at this point and congregants are aspersed with the animal's blood. If it does not, the remaining alcohol is poured out into a bowl, the Gods are thanked and the offerings poured out in the appropriate place. The rite is then closed. In an article published in the *Midsummer Thiubok* in 2001, Heathen Garman Lord writes:

> *Blóting* reminds us of the cycle of life, and that death is a vital part of nourishing our existence. By sharing in this act we re-connect with nature and develop rapport with the Gods, sharing food and common experience, the cycle of life with them. This process links us to our past and the future.[71]

That is the stated purpose of *blót*, but the actual experience within Heathenry appears far more complex. Whereas Walter Burkert postulated that the shedding of blood serves as "a striking metaphor of ... growth," in the case of modern *blót*, it often seems to serve the opposite purpose: blood is shed so that the religion, one's luck, one's life and spiritual understanding will not change.[72] Reconstructionist religions are, by their very nature, conservative in the extreme. In a religious setting that draws its inspiration primarily from pre-Christian historical and religious texts, this is to be expected. Change occurs slowly and sacrificial rituals are performed not so much to invite the Gods in, but to ensure cultural and religious stability. We have explored this point in the last chapter with reference to author James Coulter and his book

[71] Daniel O'Halloran, personal communication with author, March 12, 2002. O'Halloran trained under Garman Lord.

[72] Walter Burkert, *Creation of the Sacred* (Cambridge: Harvard University Press, 1996), 14.

Germanic Heathenry,[73]and Swain Wodening's listing of the focal points of *blót* —community, ancestors, and Gods.[74]

This ambivalence regarding *blót* highlights a greater ambivalence within the Heathen community: the ongoing ideological battle between orthodox theology and the impact of personal gnosis. To this author's mind, it also highlights the struggle of reconstructing and reviving an indigenous religious tradition in a cultural milieu dramatically different from the one in which the religion initially evolved. There is a lack of continuity that first generation converts struggle with. This becomes apparent not only in the way in which they often cling to fundamentalism as a means of defining themselves and their religion and navigating the world around them, but also in the rigid ritual structure and the fear that religious rituals might deviate or evolve from that which is noted in "lore".

This approach to the Gods within Heathenry is tinged not only with dread but also with a certain distaste. This has led one Neo-Pagan to dismiss most branches of Heathenry as "...a weird and rather sacrilegious form of ancestor worship. We'll worship our ancestors by pretending to practice their religion and worship their Gods."[75] While cynical, this comment does illustrate one of the ideological fault lines within the modern religious movement where practitioners will often happily honor their ancestors and celebrate their community, but balk at the idea of developing a deep relationship with any of their Gods. The very idea of Gods and Goddesses, of Deities active and independent in the way that the surviving myths demonstrate, is at the very least, an awkward idea for modern practitioners.

At the same time, Heathenry is seeing a slow evolution of ritual structure. Twenty years ago, sacrificial *blót* was unheard of. The importance of this type of *blót*, the care with which it must

---

[73] James Coulter, *Germanic Heathenry* (Texas: First Books Library, 2003), 154.

[74] Wodening, *Hammer of the Gods,* 127.

[75] Joshua Tenpenny, personal communication with author, September 19, 2006.

be performed, and the fact that a life is being given up to the Gods has had the effect of making the overall community far more mindful of the sacredness of its religious ritual. The power of *blót* and the growing number of people who have witnessed one has led to more Heathens discussing the possible impact of ritual. This has slowly led to a gradual increase in acceptance of personal gnosis. It has also led to more care and preparation in the ritual process, thanks in part to the care shown to the sacrificial animal in surviving accounts of lore. This awareness of the importance of sacrifice is creeping into other Reconstructionist religions as well. The first goat offering to Artemis in the modern age was performed by a Greek Reconstructionist[76] on September 2, 2006. It is worth noting that so controversial was this act that the officiating priest had to go outside of her religious community to hold the ritual.

Essentially, the body of religions that constitute the contemporary Northern Tradition are evolving through the development of ritual, which in itself has begun to evolve through the active experience of its participants. The act of sacrifice is a vital and vibrant part of this evolution. The experience of the sacred and the experience of the community partaking of the sacred has become a powerful undercurrent in the ongoing community battle between "lore" and "UPG", which is at its heart a battle between textual authority, orthodoxy and the authority of

---

[76] Greek Reconstructionist Polytheism, commonly called *Hellenismos*, is less than twenty years into its revival. It is less organized than Heathenry, but equally focused on lore to the sometimes exclusion of personal gnosis. The devotee of Artemis who offered the goat sacrifice mentioned above, had to do it on the land of a Northern Tradition shaman. The majority of *Hellenistai*, practitioners of Hellenismos, denied her the right to perform the sacrifice, arguing that while it is known sacrifice was performed to Artemis, not enough lore survives to know precisely how. Particularly lacking was information on rites of cleanliness before and after the actual killing. The woman in question felt strongly through personal gnosis that Artemis wished such a sacrifice and sought help outside of her religious community.

personal practice. These are the factors that may come to change the face of the community's *habitus* and by extension the community itself. At the heart of it all lies the archetype of the sacred king, embodied in the shaman-king God, Odin.

Bibliography

Agamben, Giorgio. *Homo Sacer*. California: Stanford University Press, 1998.

Asad, Talal. *Formations of the Secular*. California: Stanford University Press, 2003.

Auden, W.H. et al. *Norse Poems*. UK: Thetford Press, Ltd., 1981.

Bellows, Henry. *The Poetic Edda*. New York: The American Scandinavian Foundation, 1926.

Burkert, Walter. *Creation of the Sacred*. MA: Harvard University Press, 1996.

Burkert, Walter. *Homo Necans*. CA: University of California Press, 1983.

Coulter, James. *Germanic Heathenry*. TX: First Books Library, 2003.

Dubois, Thomas. *Nordic Religions in the Viking Age*. Pennsylvania: University of Pennsylvania Press, 1999.

Durkheim, Emile. *Elementary Forms of Religious Life*. UK: Oxford University Press, 2001.

Eliade, Mircea. *Shamanism: Archaic Techniques of Ecstasy*. Princeton: Princeton University Press, 1964.

Frazer, James. *The Golden Bough*. NY: The MacMillan Company, 1958.

Girard, Rene. *Violence and the Sacred*. Baltimore: John Hopkins University Press, 1977.

Glucklich, Ariel. *Sacred Pain*. UK: Oxford University Press, 2001.

Green, Miranda. *Dying for the Gods*. UK: Tempus Books, 2002.

Grönbech, Vilhelm. *Culture of the Teutons, vol. 1*. Denmark: University of Cophenhagen, 1931.

Hulsman, K. C. *Heathen Magicoreligious Practices: From the Ancient Past Through the Reconstructed Present.* Texas: University of Texas at Arlington, 2004.

Jones, Prudence & Pennick, Nigel. *A History of Pagan Europe.* London: Routledge Press, 1995.

Kaldera, Raven. *Dark Moon Rising: Pagan BDSM and the Ordeal Path.* MA: Asphodel Press, 2006.

Kaldera, Raven. *Wightridden: Paths of Northern Tradition Shamanism.* MA: Asphodel Press, 2009.

Kershaw, Kris. *The One Eyed God.* Washington, D.C.: Journal of Indo-European Studies Monograph No. 36 (2000).

Krasskova, Galina. *Exploring the Northern Tradition.* New Jersey: New Page Books, 2005.

The Life and Death of Kormak the Skald. Translated by W.G. Collingwood and J. Stefansson. The Online Medieval and Classical Library. <http://sunsite.berkeley.edu/OMACL/ Cormac/>

Lindow, John. *Norse Mythology.* UK: Oxford University Press, 2001.

Livingston, James. *Anatomy of the Sacred.* NJ: Pearson Prentice Hall, 2005.

Magnusson, Magnus et al. (translator). *Seven Viking Romances.* UK: Penguin Books, 1980.

Mauss, Marcel. *The Gift.* NY: W. W. Norton, 1990.

Robertson-Smith, William. *Lectures on the Religion of the Semites.* Elibron Classics Series, London, 2005.

Robinson, B. A. "Asatru." *Religious Tolerance: World Religions,* 1997. <http://www.religioustolerance.org/asatru.htm>.

Simek, Rudolf. *Dictionary of Northern Mythology.* UK: St. Edmundsbury Press, Ltd, 1993.

Sturluson, Snorri. "Yngling Saga." In *Heimskringla. Translated by* Lee M. Hollander. University of Texas Press, 1991.

--- "Hakon the Good's Saga." In *Heimskringla.* Trans. Lee M. Hollander . University of Texas Press.

Sigfusson, Saegmund. "Havamal." *Poetic Edda*. Trans. Benjamin Thorpe. The Erickson Family Web Site. <http://www.glenreva.com/history/lineTwo/elderEddaOdin.htm>

Tacitus, Cornelius. *The Agricola and Germania*. Edited by James Rives. Translated by Harold Mattingly. London: Penguin Books, 1948.

Turville-Petre, E.O.G. *Myth and Religion of the North*. Connecticut: Greenwood Press, 1975.

Wodening, Swain. *Hammer of the Gods*. Texas: Booksurge Press, 2003.

The Demonization of Loki

Norse mythology, as reflected in the Prose and Poetic Eddas—stories recorded one hundred years after the close of the last Heathen Temple in Uppsala, Sweden in 1100 C.E.—is replete with dynamic, inter-related families of Gods and Goddesses. Their dramas, exploits and behaviors reflect a curious panoply of conflicting elements that at times seem both ambivalent and even amoral. This is especially true of Loki. Loki is a fascinating figure. Perhaps no other being in the Northern pantheons of gods is quite so controversial and at the same time quite so compelling. This holds true not only in the scholarly world, but also within modern Heathenry or Asatru, the modern Reconstructionist faith that seeks to revive the worship of the Norse Gods. The role of Loki in this modern religious movement has created an ideological fault line that remains explosive and hotly contested within the United States' community, for just as scholars often don't seem to know what to make of this particular figure, neither does modern Asatru.

Perhaps it is fitting, given Loki's often provocative role in the Eddic lore, that a consensus within both the scholarly and religious communities as to his function and nature has yet to be truly reached. Religious historian William Paden notes that "religions are grounded in mythic language ... myth is not a medium of neutral, mathematical objectivity, but a definitive voice that names the ultimate powers that create, maintain, and re-create one's life." [1] Myths shape and define that which is ephemeral and timeless, creating living bridges to the numinous. To some extent, by their very nature, such myths also reflect the beliefs and world view of those creating them. This makes the appearance of Loki, in a mythos otherwise focused around what are known as the *Reginn*, or ordered powers, all the more thought-provoking. Frank Stanton Cawley, in his essay "The Figure of Loki in Germanic Mythology", notes that in the study

---

[1] William Paden, *Religious Worlds* (Boston: Beacon Press, 1994), 73.

of Germanic mythology, the scholar is presented with many difficult problems. "One of the most puzzling of all is that presented by the God Loki, about whose essential nature there are almost as many opinions as there are scholars who have occupied themselves with him." [2]

For that, and for his dominant role in the surviving mythos, Loki is a fascinating figure. He enlivens the Eddic tales and serves as a catalyst for both adventure and trouble. He is both friend of the Aesir and their bitterest enemy. He is numbered amongst the Gods, and yet at Ragnarok battles against them. He defies boundaries, and his apparent and uncompromising liminality presents a continuous challenge to those who would understand his nature. One modern devotee of Loki refers to him as a God of both "paradox and uncertainty". [3] That perfectly reflects the startling ambiguity with which he was equally held, not only by medieval Christian authors, who saw in him a Nordic version of Satan, but also by modern Heathens and modern scholars.

This chapter will seek to explore the nature of Loki, both his role in the surviving Eddic tales and the impact his controversial nature has had on the development of modern Heathenry (Asatru) within the United States. Loki's nature and relationship to the other Gods will be examined particularly in light of the core cosmological principles reflected in Norse beliefs both ancient and modern, and the development of a subsection of American Heathenry focused around worship of Loki and his kin will be examined.

Part I: The Role of Loki in the Eddas

According to Heathen cosmology, the world began with what amounts to a "big bang". In the beginning there existed a great chasm called Ginungagap. Scholar Rudolf Simek notes that the

---

[2] Frank Stanton Cawley, *The Figure of Loki in Germanic Mythology* (Cambridge: Harvard University Press), 310.

[3] Fuensenta Plaza, personal communication with author, April 20, 2007.

meaning of Ginungagap is "difficult to interpret etymologically" but offers either "yawning void" or, drawing on the work of Germanic scholar de Vries, "void filled with magical and creative powers." [4] Within this void lay two diametrically opposed worlds: Muspellheim, the world of fire and Niflheim, the world of ice, fog and stillness. Eventually these two worlds collided; from that elemental conflagration, life burst into being and the process of cosmic evolution began. From the primordial ooze created by the steam, ice, fog and heat, there arose the first being, a proto-giant named Ymir. Ymir was born when the ice of Niflhem melted in the heat caused by the nearness of Muspelheim. Ymir nourished himself on the milk of a primordial cow named Audhumla (from *audbr*: "riches, wealth"). [5] Audhumla in turn lived on salt, which she licked from the ice and brine of Niflheim.

As Audhumla licked the salty brine–matter that was infused with creative life force, a new being began to emerge. This was Buri. Eventually, Buri would father the first Bor, who in turn fathered the first of the Gods, including Odin. [6] Odin with his two brothers slew Ymir and from his corpse fashioned the world of man, Midgard. From the very beginning, the Aesir defined the boundaries of their worlds by the slaughter of the Jotnar, the race of Ymir's descendents from which Loki sprang. This dynamic of conflict and violence permeates the Eddic tales and lies at the heart of Loki's contentious and ambivalent nature.

Despite the fact that Odin himself traces his lineage from the Jotnar, throughout the Eddic tales, the Aesir remained in constant conflict with them. Scholars argue about the nature of the Jotnar, much as they do about the nature of the most famous member of that tribe, Loki. Many differing theories have been advanced. Some consider them personifications of the forces of nature,

---

[4] Rudolf Simek, *Dictionary of Northern Mythology* (Suffolk, UK: St. Edmundsbury Press, Ltd.), 109.

[5] Simek, *Dictionary of Northern Mythology,* 22.

[6] Galina Krasskova, *Exploring the Northern Tradition* (New Jersey: New Page Books, 2005), 28.

others an earlier group of Gods dispossessed by newer deities and therefore hostile to them.[7] This theory is occasionally espoused by followers of the *Rökkr* movement in modern Asatru, a fringe movement that focuses not on worship of the Aesir or Vanir, but rather on worship of the Jotnar. Loki is simply the most obvious of the Aesir's links to the more violent and primal world of the giants, standing—as one scholar noted—"midway between the doomed gods and the hostile powers which ultimately compass their destruction.[8]

According to the primary sources, at some point in their early history, Loki and Odin became blood-brothers. In stanza nine of the *Lokasenna*, Loki reminds Odin:

Remember, Othin, in olden days
That we both our blood have mixed;
Then didst thou promise no ale to pour,
Unless it were brought to us both. [9]

This connection to Odin persists, carrying over even into English folk charms down into the 19th century. The connection also, inextricable as it seems to be, has caused some scholars to dismiss Loki as nothing more than a hypostasis of Odin.[10] In fact, that is one of three primary explications of Loki's nature; the others being that he is a Fire God and a Trickster Deity. Additionally, Georges Dumezil considered Loki, falling as he does outside of the tri-partite Divine functions, as being an incarnation of impulsive intelligence.[11] In order to draw any conclusions as to

---

[7] John MacCulloch, *Mythology of All Races, Vol. 2* (New York: Cooper Square Publishers, 1964), 281.

[8] Cawley, *The Figure of Loki in Germanic Mythology,* 311.

[9] Snorri Sturluson, *The Poetic Edda,* trans. Henry Bellows (New York: The American Scandinavian Foundation, 2003), 155.

[10] Stefanie Von Schnurbein, "The Function of Loki in Snorri Sturluson's Edda." *History of Religions* vol. 40, no. 2 (November, 2000), 113.

[11] Georges Dumezil, *Loki* (France: Flammarion, 1986), 216.

the validity of each of these theories, it is necessary to discuss the manner in which Loki actually appears in the origin literature.

Loki is the child of two Jotnar: Laufey ("Leafy Isle") and Farbauti ("Cruel-Striker"). His mother is sometimes also referred to as Nal ("Needle") and apparently has two other sons: Byleistr and Helblindi, about which nothing else is known. Loki is often known as Laufeysson, and has several other bynames or *heiti*, including Lopt ("Airy One" or "Lightening One") [12] "Bound God", "Wolf's Father" (referring to his siring of the great wolf Fenris), "Sly One" and "the Foe of the Gods".[13] Some attempts have been made to link him with Loður, third in the divine triune of Odin, Hoenir and Loður, but there is no etymological basis for this connection.

Loki has two wives, as different as night from day to each other. The first is a sorceress of the ironwood named Angrboda ("one who brings grief") by which he sired a brood of "monsters": Fenris, the wolf of chaos, Jormungand, the world serpent and Hela, who became the Goddess of the Underworld. The Gods were so threatened by these three children that they banished them. Fenris was bound, Jormungand was tossed into the ocean and set to encircle Midgard and Hela was cast into the land of the Dead. Loki's second wife, Sigyn, was ostensibly of the Aesir, though nothing about her background is known. Her name means "victory woman" and every reference made to her in the Eddas (of which there are only three) refers to her loyalty to Loki. After his part in the death of Baldr, he was bound in a cave with a poisonous serpent fixed above his head. Sigyn refused to repudiate him and stood by his side loyally holding a bowl to catch the venom that the serpent dripped onto him. It is known that he had two sons by her—Narvi and Vali—but when he was bound, it was with the entrails of his own son, as Vali was turned into a wolf by the Aesir and in turn killed his brother.

---

[12] Simek, *Dictionary of Northern Mythology*, 195.

[13] MacCulloch, *Mythology of All Races*, 147.

Loki is responsible for the Gods gaining many of their most powerful tools from Odin's spear to Thor's hammer. There are several episodes in the Edda where Loki functions as a thief. In one of these escapades, he sneaks into the bedroom of Sif, wife of the Thunder God Thor, and cuts off all her hair. This was a grave insult and humiliation in Nordic culture, being a punishment visited on adulterous women. Thor is, of course, enraged, and in the face of his fury, Loki offers to put things right. In order to do so, Loki travels to Nidavellir, the land of the Duergar—dwarves renowned for their skill in smithcraft. He finagled and bartered and convinced the dwarves to craft new hair out of pure gold for Sif, a wig that when placed upon her shorn head would take root and grow like real hair, becoming more beautiful than the original. He also had them craft other gifts to make up for his transgression. He goaded two different dwarven clans into a contest, betting his head against the original crafter Brokk that Brokk would lose this contest. Of course, he did not: the winning gift, out of several which included Odin's spear Gungnir and Frey's ship Skidbladnir, was Mjolnir the Hammer of Thor. Loki didn't lose his head, however, as he pointed out that he hadn't bet any part of his neck. Brokk had to content himself with sewing the Jotun's lips closed instead.

Loki was also indirectly responsible for the theft of Idunna's apples. Idunna was guardian of the apples of youth, for the Norse Gods are neither immortal nor unchanging. On one of his travels, Loki was captured by the giant Thjiazi and in order to secure his escape, he promised to bring Idunna and her precious apples to Thjiazi. He contrived for Idunna to be captured, and only when the Gods began to age did he admit his part in her disappearance and work to gain her return. This he did by borrowing Freya's shapeshifting falcon cloak, flying into Thjiazi's stronghold, transforming Idunna into a nut and flying back to Asgard with her thus transformed in his claws. The chase, however, led to the death of Thjiazi, and eventually to his daughter Skaði storming Asgard demanding wergild for her father's death. Loki helped ameliorate her anger in that instance by debasing himself to make her laugh, but ultimately Skaði was to have her vengeance on Laufey's son.

Loki was also known to be somewhat fluid in his gender presentation, and this is one of his attributes that has caused some scholars, like de Vries, to classify him as a Trickster figure. It is certainly one of the major issues modern Asatruar have with this most changeable of Gods, the other being Loki's role in the death of Odin's favorite son Baldr.

Part II: Loki as a Trickster Figure

One of the most enduring theories about Loki's nature is that he is the quintessential Trickster figure. While this theory is not without controversy, it does provide an interesting avenue into the examination of Loki's character. Lewis Hyde, in his book *Trickster Makes the World*, defines a Trickster Deity as one who represents the "paradoxical category of sacred amorality."[14] He goes on to point out that Tricksters invariably appear in nearly every mythology, often cropping up in folklore and popular culture as well:

> Every group has its edge, its sense of in and out, and trickster is always there, at the gates of the city and the gates of life, making sure there is commerce. He also attends the internal boundaries by which groups articulate their social life. We constantly distinguish—right and wrong, sacred and profane, clean and dirty, male and female, young and old, living and dead—and in every case Trickster will cross the line and confuse the distinction ...Trickster is the

---

[14] Lewis Hyde, *Trickster Makes the World* (New York: North Point Press, 1998), 10.

mythic embodiment of ambiguity and ambivalence, doubleness and duplicity, contradiction and paradox.[15]

Because Tricksters are defined by their ambiguity and guile, it is not surprising then to find folklorists and scholars willing to place Loki in this category.[16] Like the West African Eshu, Loki may be considered a trickster not only "because he fools people and creates chaos, but because he's always escaping the codes of the world."[17] Dumezil, for instance, in his monograph *Loki*, while not approaching Loki as a Trickster, discusses him as a manifestation of creative and often impulsive intelligence, what he calls "the unquiet thought".[18] Scholar Jan de Vries, on the other hand, places Loki definitively in the category of Trickster, emphasizing his nature as mischief maker,[19] and equating him with Loður as a divine thief of fire. Dumezil also makes this comparison:

> It is admitted by all scholars that the most outstanding feature of Loki is his character as a trickster and a thief. With only very few exceptions all the traditions about him show him as a cunning creature, delighting in making mischief. Sometimes he shows a rather childish pleasure in playing his tricks upon the gods, often he contrives to do serious damage, but in most cases he is obliged to repair his faults. ...Loki as a trickster is quite sufficient as a religious phenomenon.[20]

---

[15] Ibid., 7

[16] Ibid., 18

[17] Erik Davis, "Trickster at the Crossroads" *Gnosis 19* (1991), 39.

[18] Dumezil, *Loki,* 216.

[19] Jan de Vries, *The Problem of Loki.* (Helsinki: Suomalainen Tiedeakatemia, 1933), 224.

[20] Ibid., 253-254.

Parallels may also be drawn between Loki as Trickster and Loki, Prometheus-like, as a cultural hero. Something of this perhaps survives in the Faroese balled, the *Loka Táttur,* in which Loki is the only God out of three (the others being Odin and Hoenir) who is able to save a peasant boy from a giant's wrath. This tale stands in stark relief amongst the surviving lore, portraying Loki as a cultural hero instead of as the enemy of Gods and man.

The Trickster and the Hero are both powerful cultural archetypes often highlighting those transformative or traumatic moments where the sacred leaks into everyday life. The most ubiquitous of mythic or archetypal figures are often also the most disturbing and controversial, and the trickster is no exception to this rule. Diana Paxson in her book *Essential Asatru* declares: "Steer clear of Loki if you have problems with ambiguity"; and later notes that "...like Coyote in Native American myth, Loki is a trouble maker and a culture bringer, the latter often as a result of the former."[21]

As Hyde notes, Tricksters are Gods of uncertainty.[22] They are figures who "can tear a hole in the fabric of fate so a person might slip from one life into another."[23]They help the outsider escape the restrictions and boundaries imposed by cultural conventions. Liminal figures, tricksters often define thresholds and then by their actions either cross or expand those thresholds. Tricksters inhabit "the cracks between languages or between heaven and earth,"[24] and by their finagling machinations, create a means whereby diametrically opposed opposites (like heaven and earth, good and evil, chaos and order) may intersect and learn from each other without actually touching and thereby violating the

---

[21] Diana Paxson, *Essential Asatru* (New York: Citadel Press, 2006), 71.

[22] Hyde, *Trickster Makes the World,* 247.

[23] Ibid.

[24] Hyde, *Trickster Makes the World,* 260.

necessary boundary between the sacred and profane.[25]They are the enemies of entropy, the living embodiment that unchanging surety is an illusion—that, as the Greek philosopher Heraclitus said: *Everything changes. Nothing remains the same.* [26]

Like any good trickster, Loki is the most controversial being in the entire Nordic pantheon. Many modern Asatruar won't even utter his name, such is the discomfort he inspires. Loki entered the ordered ranks of the Aesir through a "back door", so to speak; he swore blood brotherhood with Odin (a God with more than his fair share of tricksterish qualities). This oath entitled Loki to be treated with all the honor and respect due to Odin's actual brother.[27] Despite this erstwhile acceptance into the ranks of the Aesir, Loki pays little heed to their rules and comfort zones. Interestingly enough, one possible etymology of Loki's name is "a looped piece of string"; in other words, a loop-hole.[28] Certainly in the surviving Eddic tales, Loki is a master of creating them both for himself and others.

It is part of a trickster's nature that they force those who work with them to expand the boundaries of their understanding. They bring evolution, a dynamic synergy and creative power. They often act as catalysts and facilitators of growth. Through Loki's tricks, for instance, the Gods acquire tools like Mjolnir that help them defend and maintain the order that the Aesir had created at the beginning of time. When Thor's hammer is later stolen, it is through Loki's quick thinking that Thor is able to win it back.[29]

---

[25] Ibid., 63.

[26] Maurice Balme, et al, *Athenaze: An Introduction to Ancient Greek.* (New York: Oxford University Press, 2003), 11.

[27] Krasskova, *Exploring the Northern Tradition*, 97.

[28] "Viking Baby Names" Ellipsis, <http://www.ellipsis.cx/-liana/names/norse/vikbynames.html>.

[29] As will be discussed in detail below, a certain gender fluidity is also often the mark of a trickster, and it is notable that in the *Thrymskiviða*, Thor must disguise himself as the goddess Freya to triumph. Loki himself exhibits a certain ambiguity in the area of gender, even transforming into female form twice, once actually giving birth.

At the same time, through Loki's direct interference, the Gods lose Baldr, one of the favored sons of Odin. Eventually, Loki is said to rise up against the Gods.

So what are the traditional characteristics of a trickster, outside of a certain moral ambiguity? Folklorist Barbara Babcock defines trickster figures by their duality:

> No figure in literature, oral or written, baffles us quite as much as trickster. He is positively identified with creative powers, often bringing such defining features of culture as fire or basic food, and yet he constantly behaves in the most antisocial manner we can imagine. Although we laugh at him for his troubles and his foolishness and are embarrassed by his promiscuity, his creative cleverness amazes us and keeps alive the possibility of transcending the social restrictions we regularly encounter ...In the majority of his encounters with men, he violates rules or boundaries, thereby necessitating escape and forcing himself to again wander aimlessly...
>
> Trickster is ... a "creative negation" who introduces death and with it all possibilities to the world ... Things "are" by virtue of and in relation to what they "are not": structure implies antistructure and cannot exist without it. ...Trickster, "the foolish one"—the negation offering possibility—stands in immediate relation to the center in all its ambiguity ... And for this we not only tolerate this "margin of mess", this "enemy of boundaries", we create and re-create him. [30]

---

[30] Barbara Babcock Abrahams, "A Tolerated Margin of Mess: The Trickster and His Tales Reconsidered." *Journal of the Folklore Institute, 11, no. 3 (1975): 147-186.*

It is easy to see Loki fitting into these rather broad categories. He is bringer of gifts, cultural hero, and at the same time brings destruction (or negation) by helping to kill Baldr and eventually leading the Jotnar forces against the Aesir at Ragnarok. Erin Weber in her article on Nanabozho and Hermes briefly discusses the attributes common to tricksters across cultures, again reinforcing their ambivalent ambiguity:

> [G]odlike qualities intermixed with human frailties, the role of educator, often through the counter or negative example (particularly through ambiguous sexuality that presents the consequences of disobedience vis-à-vis societal norms), as well as the function of guide to worlds unknown or as middleman or conductor between worlds. In essence, the trickster embodies an entire bundle of contradictions that enact an uneasy but necessary reconciliation of the world's dualities. [31]

Loki, a being who resists categorization of any sort, manages to fall fairly neatly into the categories that define tricksters. A few relevant examples will clearly highlight this aspect of Loki's nature.

Creative Powers, Bringer of Culture

As discussed above, Loki was responsible for the acquisition of several important tools of the other Gods. In payment for his theft of Sif's hair, he won Mjolnir, the hammer by which Thor defends Midgard and the realm of the Gods against Jotun incursion; Odin's armring Draupnir that drops eight identical rings every ninth night; Frey's golden boar Gullinbursti—and of course, Sif received new hair made entirely of gold, hair that took root and

---

[31] Erin Weber, "Nanabozho and Hermes: A Look at the Persistence of the Trickster Archetype in Louise Erdrich's *Tracks* and Thomas Mann's *Death in Venice*." (M.A. thesis, Middle Tennesee University, 2006), 74.

grew like real hair when placed upon her shorn head. The theft of Sif's hair and its eventual replacement with pure gold is interesting in that many modern Heathens (and some scholars) accept the idea that her hair represented the grain crop (particularly wheat). This story may be symbolic of the seasonal harvest—the grain, so necessary for life, is cut and grows anew with the turning of seasons. Scholar Marion Ingham points out that the few scholars who still support such nature-symbolism point to the fact that it is virtually indispensable to have thunderstorms for the grain to ripen—it fixes the nitrogen—and Thor with his mighty hammer is associated with thunder.[32] Thus, in a rather round-about way (fitting for a trickster), Loki might be seen to assist in bringing about the creative abundance of the harvest.

Loki is associated with fire and by some scholars (such as de Vries) with Loður, one of the triune of creator Gods (the other two being Odin and Hoenir). Of Loður, the *Voluspa* notes that he was responsible for bestowing "life hue and warmth" upon the first man and woman, just as Odin gave breath, and Hoenir consciousness:

Önd þau né áttu,
óð þau né höfðu,
lá né laeti,
né litu góða.
Önd gaf Haenir,
lá gaf Lóður
og litu góða.[33]

Of course it should be noted that not all scholars accept Loki and Loður as being the same entity. There is admittedly scant etymological evidence to support this attribution, yet the translation of the name as "Fire bringer" and Loki's ongoing

---

[32] Krasskova, *Exploring the Northern Tradition*, 53.

[33] *Eddukvaeði*, trans. Gísli Sigurðsson,(Reykjavik: Mál og Menning, 1999), 9.

84   GALINA KRASSKOVA

connection with fire, particularly in folklore where he is often
regarded as something of a fire-spirit or fire demon, as well as
Loki's connections with Odin, have contributed to its
persistence.[34]

By some accounts, Loki creates the fishnet, which is then
used to trap him when he attempts to flee in the aftermath of the
Lokasenna. Then there is the story of Skrymsli the peasant's child
in which Loki is hailed as a hero, providing a permanent solution
to the danger the child was in, where Odin and Hoenir only
provided temporary aid.[35] And while it may not fall strictly within
the confines of "culture-bringer", in his travels with Thor, Loki
does consistently help his companion navigate interactions with
the Jotnar, effectively bridging two disparate cultures.

Promiscuity and sexual ambiguity

Perhaps no other aspect of Loki's character gives modern
scholars and Asatruar such pause as his sexual exploits and
ambiguity. Unlike any other God, Loki is known to several times
have shape shifted into female form. While Odin is accused of
unmanly behavior and keeping company with witches in the
Lokasenna, only Loki goes so far as to assume female shape. He
first does so when the safety of Asgard is under threat. A
stonemason hires out to the Aesir to build a sturdy protective wall
around Asgard. His payment, should he finish by a set date, was to
be the sun, moon and Freya as his bride. The Aesir agreed largely
because it did not seem possible for the giant to finish in the time
allotted. The giant's magical horse Svadilfari, however, proves to
be of more aid than the Gods expected, so to lure the stallion away
and thus slow the giant down to prevent him from fulfilling his
part of the contract, Loki transforms into a mare and seduces
Svadilfari away. This results in Loki giving birth to Odin's eight-

---

[34] MacCulloch, *Mythology of All Races*, 148-149.

[35] H. A. Guerber, *The Norsemen* (UK: Senate Publishing Company, 1994), 119.

legged steed Sleipnir, hailed in the *Grimnismal* as "the best of horses".

He again transformed into female form (this time that of an old woman) after the death of Baldr. Hela, Mistress of the Underworld, had agreed to release Baldr from her realm on the condition that every living thing weep for him. In the guise of the old woman Thokk, Loki refused, saying "Let Hel keep what she has." He is also accused of taking the form of a milkmaid and living for eight winters beneath the earth and bearing children.[36] Preben Sorenson speculates that this "must certainly be taken to mean that Loki served as mistress to giants or trolls, whose sexuality was considered gross and unbridled."[37] He points out that in Nordic culture, "the charge of wearing women's clothes, of performing women's work or being a woman or a female animal evoked the whole complex of ideas on cowardice and effeminacy" (when applied to men).[38] Thus, Loki taking the form of a woman was in effect, Loki violating a major cultural taboo and engaging in that which was *nið* and/or *argr* ("forbidden" or "gender-crossing").

Transcendence of social restrictions/violation of boundaries

This is perhaps the area in which Loki most exemplifies tricksterish behavior. Most glaringly evident are his violations of gender and sexuality taboos as noted above. Loki manifested through his gender fluidity, behavior that was considered *nið* and/or *argr*—unmanly and effeminate and thus inappropriate. It is worthy to note that many modern Asatruar find this particular behavior equally as offensive as his role in the death of Baldr.

Gender fluidity aside, the very means by which Loki becomes part of Aesir society exemplifies his position as "other". He is of Jotun birth, a member of a race in constant conflict with the Aesir,

---

[36] *Lokasenna*, stanza 23.

[37] Sorenson, 24.

[38] Ibid.

yet he becomes blood brother to Odin and thus gains entrance into that culture. He travels frequently between the two worlds, maintaining a wife amongst the Aesir (Sigyn) and a wife amongst the Jotnar (Angurboða). On the latter, he births three terrifying children: Fenris, the great wolf of chaos who so frightens the Aesir that they contrive to bind him; Jormungand, a great serpent who is thrown into the sea to surround Midgard; and Hela, a half woman-half corpse child, who is cast into the Underworld to become its ruler. On Sigyn, Loki fathers two boys, Narvi and Vali, but one is killed by his brother who is transformed into a wolf when Loki is bound. So while Loki brings very helpful tools to the Aesir and utilizes his cunning intelligence to help them avoid trouble (or conversely to get them out of trouble that he has helped create), he also sires children who embody the powers of destruction, transformation, and death.

Loki is a thief; by that very definition he is a violator of boundaries. He steals Freya's necklace as well as Sif's hair, and is the cause of Idunna and her apples of youthfulness being stolen by the giant Thjiazi. In this latter story, Loki manages to rescue Idunna, which leads to Thjiazi being killed. This in turn leads to Thjiazi's daughter Skaði storming the halls of the Aesir demanding wergild for the death of her father. Loki assists in soothing her anger, playing the fool to cause her to laugh. This he achieves by tying the beard of a goat to his testicles and prancing around, in yet another example of sexually ambiguous behavior. By setting into motion the course of events that led to Skaði allying herself with the Aesir, Loki crossed yet another boundary and helped bring some of the wildness and primal power of the Jotun race into the sacred enclosure of Asgard.

Loki was also known for his shapeshifting, which is perhaps the most concrete and pragmatic of his violations of accepted boundaries. At various times he transformed into a mare (birthing Sleipnir), a seal (battling with Heimdall after his theft of Brisingamen), a fly (on two occasions), a flea, a milkmaid, a woman, a giantess, and a salmon. He also borrowed Freya's feathered cloak to transform into a bird to retrieve Idunna.[39] These exploits violate not only simple physical boundaries but also gender expectations, as noted above.

Creative negation/introduction of death/possibilities

While he is not ever associated with being a death deity in and of himself, Loki hovers on the periphery of death and transformation throughout the Eddic lore. Firstly, he is the father of Hela, who takes her place in the Nordic pantheon as the Goddess of the Underworld. Secondly, in contributing to the death of Baldr, Loki becomes a bringer of death and opens up the possibility of the order the Gods created surviving Ragnarok, for after Ragnarok, Baldr is freed from Hel and thus something of the world of the Gods remains intact.

Loki is clearly a liminal figure, always existing betwixt and between: neither fully part of the world of the Jotnar (beings of Nature and chaos) nor fully part of the world of the Gods. Belonging to neither, he is able to move between both and possesses the synergetic power of active manifestation. Because he is a being of chaos yet bound to order via his oath to Odin, he is able to manifest this quixotic and change-inducing power directly in the ordered realm of the Gods. He opens careful doorways and through them, that power is brought under tentative control. This liminality is perhaps the most ambivalent aspect of Loki's nature, as it is within many tricksters, though the most cursory examination of the surviving literature shows that Odin possesses it as well. Odin, however, always returns to the secure realm of *inangarð*, to the hallowed ground of the Gods. Loki is never part of that, though he may dwell there for awhile. He is always an outsider, always on the fringe of the Divine community, always "other". [40]

---

[39] MacCulloch, *Mythology of All Races,* 146.

[40] Krasskova, *Exploring the Northern Tradition*, 99.

Because, as the stories of Loki show, tricksters are never actually fully accepted parts of the communities they serve, they provide unique role models for those people who may struggle with the artificial and often limiting boundaries of their culture or society. Tricksters help humanity recognize and effectively utilize those opportunities whereby cultural conventions may be usurped or surmounted or simply dispensed with entirely. The struggle to overcome and better one's fate is a recurring theme in many myths, from that of Prometheus stealing fire to aid humankind to Sigurd, battling the vagaries and often brutal implacability of *Wyrd*. Myth encapsulates that eternal struggle and the trickster teachers various methods whereby one might triumph at it. Hyde refers to these methods as works of *artus* and theorizes that it is such "*artus*-working" that truly defines the trickster.[41]

Artus is a Latin word for joint, though it's also related to the word *ars* or art, skill, craft (or a crafty action).[42] The trickster possesses a singular talent for finding the point between dualities, between heaven and earth and turning reality on its proverbial head. As "*artus*-workers", tricksters ferret out hidden vulnerabilities (just as Loki found Baldr's vulnerability to the mistletoe) and untruths, utilizing the first and exposing the second. In Nordic cosmology, Loki might actually have gotten away with his part in the slaying of Baldr were it not for his visit to one of the Aesir's feasts wherein he systematically exposed the weaknesses of each God and Goddess present, pointing out where they fell short of the expectations of the Divine community (modeled, of course, on Norse ethics and mores of the time). It was this act, encapsulated in the Eddic poem the *Lokasenna*, which led to Loki's punishment, not merely his hand in killing a God.

---

[41] Hyde, *Trickster Makes the World,* 252.

[42] Ibid., 254.

Hyde notes that "trickster shifts patterns in relation to one another, and by that redefines the patterns themselves." [43] Being outside of the community, yet conversely (and to a limited degree) part of it, the trickster has a remarkable freedom not only in pointing out weaknesses, but in navigating them to his own advantage. He becomes the translator between the world of myth and the world of temporal culture, a fact that perhaps explains Loki's many appearances in Scandinavian and even Anglo-Saxon folklore.

In many respects, the trickster is a translator. Translation, the act of changing one thing into another, occurs at the point of articulation and underlies nearly all of Loki's actions. It involves both an act of sacrifice—of that which is being translated or changed—and creation. In the hands of the trickster, nothing remains untouched, unknowable, unchanging. At the same time, the trickster, who himself acts without shame, makes one ever more aware of those things society might define as shameful (often by his very violation of societal rules and boundaries). Inevitably, the trickster is punished for his transgressions against his community's taboos, and by this highlights that to be without shame is to be without reverence. It is not reverence that the trickster fights against, but unmindful, unthinking regulations that are irreverent in their lack of mindfulness, regardless of how much shame they evoke. Glimmers of this may be seen in the *Lokasenna,* wherein Loki attacks the sexual behavior of the Gods. Tricksters not only show how to circumvent the boundaries of cultural taboo, but conversely, when they should be upheld as well.

In acting the trickster, Loki is both cunning thief and provocateur, dancing merrily across the divide between the sacred and profane, shameful and honorable, accepted and taboo. As trickster, he supports the traditional structure and boundaries of their communities, and at the same time, creates doorways

---

[43] Ibid., 257.

whereby the sacred, the numinous, the unexpected—that which brings evolution—may touch and transform the community.

Part III: Loki in Modern American Heathenry

While Loki remains an ambivalent figure at best to the scholarly community, the response to him within modern Heathenry has been no less dichotic. Worship of Loki forms one of the predominant ideological fault lines within the American Heathen community, and one of the most hotly contested. (It should be noted that this article deals only with American Heathenry. Only American Heathens were interviewed for this research and the author makes no claims concerning the nature of European or Icelandic Heathenry.)

Heathenry is a Reconstructionist religion. This essentially means that practitioners strive to recreate their religion as it existed prior to the insurgence of Christianity. Historical accuracy in rites and rituals and in one's approach to the Gods is of the utmost importance to Reconstructionists. There are many other Reconstructionist religions than Heathenry; while Heathenry draws its cultural and religious impetus from Northern Europe, modern *Hellenismos* does the same with ancient Greece, as does Orthodox Kemeticism with ancient Egyptian culture and religion, for instance. One factor that every Reconstructionist religion has in common is the importance they give to what is commonly termed "the lore". Within Heathenry, this lore is comprised of the Eddas, the Sagas, Anglo-Saxon medical charms, and any and all surviving historical texts. Added to this is a plethora of modern scholarly research, linguistic analysis and anthropological study. It is from this body of work—none of which was ever intended to be utilized as religious documents—that Heathen rituals have been reconstructed, and from which modern Heathens draw their approach to the Gods.

No other God or Goddess evokes such a heated response amongst Heathens. Four people interviewed for this article felt they had been driven out of the Heathen community because of their worship of Loki, and one dedicated Loki's-woman, living in Colorado, actually received death threats from local Heathens.[44] This, however, is extreme. The majority of mainstream Heathens tend to view Loki with a mixture of respect and wariness. Diana Paxson, a well known Heathen author, writes in her book *Essential Asatru* that:

> If you want to start a "spirited" discussion among Heathens, ask whether Loki should be honored in ritual. Some, in particular those who follow the Theodish traditions, abhor him to the point where they will not allow his name to be mentioned in the hall. Others point out that he brings gifts as well as troubles and will hold a blot for him with cinnamon schnapps or peppered vodka in which you toss a dram into the fire each time you drink to him. However, you should bear in mind that Loki is a trickster, and unless you are experienced in dealing with chaotic forces, it might be better not to attract his attention.[45]

This is in stark contrast to Theodish belief, which sees him as a betrayer, liar and enemy of the Gods.[46] In fact, this is the primary issue that Heathens have with Loki: according to the Eddas, he rises up against the Gods at Ragnarok. Many cannot reconcile honor and worship of Loki with honor and worship of the rest of the Aesir, despite the fact that the *Prose Edda* clearly lists him amongst the Gods.

At the opposite end of the spectrum, there are some Heathens and Norse Pagans who focus their worship on the *Jotnar*. They often refer to themselves as *Rökkr* or *Rökkatru* from an Old Norse

---

[44] Elizabeth Vongvisith, personal communication with author, March 16, 2005.

[45] Paxson, *Essential Asatru*, 72.

[46] K.C. Hulsman, personal communication with author.

word for "shadow" or "twilight." [47] Many of these people claim experiences of Loki that stand in stark contrast to the image more conservative Heathens would present. There are even a growing number of women who have specifically devoted themselves to Loki as servants or spouses.[48] The publication of the first book of devotional poetry focused around Loki, Elizabeth Vongvisith's *Trickster, My Beloved*, occurred in 2006. Needless to say, those who claim to be *Rökkatru* or who otherwise devote themselves to Loki and his kin are not often welcomed within mainstream Heathenry.

Those who are exploring Northern Tradition neo-shamanism also work extensively with Loki and his kin, and this has aroused much controversy and hostility within Heathenry. Books like Raven Kaldera's *Jotunbok: Working with the Giants of the Northern Tradition*, which present the *Jotnar* in a positive light, are often met with vitriol. Kaldera refers to Loki as "...the most infamous Jotun of all."[49] Casey Woods, a tribalist Heathen and scholar describes the conundrum that Loki poses for the average Heathen:

> In modern day reconstructed Heathenry, Loki is a problematic God. The problem in dealing with Loki is something avoided by those Heathens who have reconstructed their practices from Anglo-Saxon sources, because the God does not appear in those sources. For all other Heathens, he is regarded in the following three ways:
>
> ❖ As the highest villain, and a great abomination against society and the other Gods in Asgard. He

---

[47] Krasskova, *Exploring the Northern Tradition*, 97.

[48] Contemporary Heathenry has also seen women devoted to Odin formalize their devotion through marriage; the same had happened with women devoted to Frey.

[49] Raven Kaldera, *Jotunbok: Working with the Giants of the Northern Tradition* (Massachusetts: Asphodel Press, 2006), 251.

should not be honored or even spoken of (especially during holy rites).

❖ With a wary respect, only afforded as a means of insurance against either Loki or Odin's wrath since Loki is Odin's oath-brother, and it is rude to honor one and not the other. This wariness also comes from Heathens not knowing clearly how to treat this God, so they err on the side of caution somewhere in the middle between the two extremes.

❖ Greatly honored and loved. For those few who honor and love Loki, and use not their devotion of him as an excuse for improper behavior, they love him whole-heartedly – although Heathens who view him in this regard, clearly acknowledge that he is a difficult God to work with, because he will not allow them to stagnate, but rather will prod them to new growths and understanding. [50]

Followers of Loki point out that he has more stories in the Norse lore than almost any other Deity, and those stories would be the poorer were he to be removed from them. They also often favor the triumvirate of Odin, Hoenir and Loki. Some, existing as they do within the liminal places of their own religious communities (either for their work within northern tradition shamanism, which is also controversial in American Heathenry, or because they violate gender or sexual taboos, or because they have been forced out of mainstream Heathenry for their work with the *Jotnar*) look to Loki as a role model, noting that:

Almost every society has been forced to create two ethical systems—an ideal one and a practical one. Pre-Christian Northern Europe was no exception.

---

[50] Casey Woods, personal communication with author, July 17, 2006.

They had a warrior code of ethics which placed a high premium on honor and honesty: without that, their civilization would soon have descended into anarchy ... and yet because they lived in a harsh and violent world, they were sometimes forced to do dishonorable things to survive. Loki's treachery is more often than not reserved for the enemies of Asgard ... Loki brings Asgard some of its most precious treasures, but often he brings them at the price of honor. [51]

In this respect, Loki's role becomes analogous to his role in the *Loka Tattur*: he is again receiving ownership over those that fall outside the boundaries of the other ordered powers. He is the God that governs all those things that fit nowhere else.[52]

It is not surprising that a Reconstructionist religion like Heathenry would find Loki's nature troublesome. Heathenry is a very conservative religion, as Reconstructionist religions tend to be. They approach the Gods with the wish that their communities should be unchanging. They look to a sometimes idealized vision of the past to craft their religion and religious community in the modern day. Whereas the more liberal denominations of Heathenry, and also Norse Paganism, utilize the surviving stories and lore to enhance a spirituality based on their own personal experiences, the traditionalists utilize lore to define and confine their religious life. Loki in many respects embodies the principle of change with all its attendant chaos and messiness. In a religion dedicated to preserving and restoring the past, it is not surprising to find that his influence is often less than welcome. Yet one must ask what is lost by the rabid exclusion of such a being. Along with change, the stories about Loki demonstrate a creative force and drive without which the tales of the Gods would be dull indeed.

---

[51] Kenaz Filan, personal communication with author, November 1, 2007.

[52] Sophie Reicher, personal communication with author, September 12, 2005.

For a religion that must balance a dedication to the past with the realities of surviving and evolving in the modern world, it seems that Loki, with his skill at navigating the knife edge precipices between uncertainties would be more needed than ever.

Loki is loved and Loki is hated within Heathenry. He commands intense respect and loyalty from those who follow Him, and yet to others within the same religion, he is regarded as the "arch enemy", a fiend and betrayer of the Gods. Scholars find him equally difficult to pin down, and he remains both a controversial figure and a fascinating one. Whether he is viewed as villain or trickster, worthy of honor or deserving only hostility, his presence in the Eddas certainly ensures that the Gods and the worlds they crossed are anything but static. With Loki in their midst, to scholars and devotees alike, the stories contained in the Eddas can never be frozen or immobile. Rather, they retain the ability to capture the imagination, fire the heart of spiritual devotion and spur, in a manner which would do Loki proud, conflict, controversy, debate and evolution.

Bibliography

Babcock-Abrahams, Barbara. "A Tolerated Margin of Mess: The Trickster and His Tales Reconsidered." *Journal of the Folklore Institute,* vol. 11, no. 3 (1975). pp. 147-186.

Balme, Maurice et al. *Athenaze: An Introduction to Ancient Greek.* New York: Oxford University Press, 2003.

Bellows, Henry. *The Poetic Edda.* New York: The American Scandinavian Foundation, 1926.

Cawley, Frank Stanton. *The Figure of Loki in Germanic Mythology.* Cambridge: Harvard University Press, 1939.

Davis, Erik. "Trickster at the Crossroads." *Gnosis Magazine,* Spring #19, 1991.

de Vries, Jan. *The Problem of Loki.* Helsinki: Suomalainen Tiedeakatemia, 1933.

Ellis-Davidson, H.R. *Gods and Myths of Northern Europe.* New York: Penguin Books, 1964.

Dumezil, Georges. *Loki*. France: Flammarion, 1986.

Guerber, H.A. *The Norsemen*. UK: Senate Publishing Company, 1994.

Hyde, Lewis. *Trickster Makes the World*. New York: North Point Press, 1998.

Kaldera, Raven. *Jotunbok: Working with the Giants of the Northern Tradition*. MA: Asphodel Press, 2006.

Krasskova, Galina. *Exploring the Northern Tradition*. New Jersey: New Page Books, 2005.

MacCulloch, John. *Mythology of All Races, Vol. 2*. New York: Cooper Square Publishers, Inc., 1964.

Paden, William. *Religious Worlds*. Boston: Beacon Press, 1994.

Paxson, Diana. *Essential Asatru*. New York: Citadel Press, 2006.

Rooth, Anna Birgitta. *Loki in Scandinavian Mythology*. Lund: C.W.K. Gleerups Förlag, 1961.

Eddukvaeði. Translated by Gísli Sigurðsson. Reykjavik, Iceland: Mál og Menning, 1999.

Sorenson, Preben. *The Unmanly Man: Concepts of Sexual Defamation in Early Northern Society*. Denmark: Odense University Press, 1983.

Simek, Rudolf. *Dictionary of Northern Mythology*. UK: St. Edmundsbury Press, Ltd., 1993.

Von Schnurbein, Stefanie. "The Function of Loki in Snorri Sturluson's Edda." *History of Religions*, vol. 40, no. 2 (November, 2000), pp. 109–124.

Weber, Erin."Nanabozho and Hermes: A Look at the Persistence of the Trickster Archetype in Louise Erdrich's *Tracks* and Thomas Mann's *Death in Venice*." M.A. thesis, Middle Tennessee University, 2006.

About The Author

Galina Krasskova has been a Heathen priest and theologian for close to twenty years. Originally ordained in 1995 through the pan-Pagan organization the Fellowship of Isis, she has also attended the Interfaith Seminary, the oldest interfaith seminary in the United States, where she received training, ordination, and certification as an interfaith minister in 2000. She took vows as a *gythia*, or Heathen priest, in 1995 and again in 2004, and is currently the Dean for second-year students at the Interfaith Seminary—the only Heathen to hold such a position to date.

Ms. Krasskova holds diplomas from The New Seminary (2000), a B.A. in Religious Studies from Empire State College (2007), and an M.A. in Religious Studies from New York University (2009). Over the years, she has presented at prestigious academic conferences including those held at Harvard, Santa Barbara University, and Ohio State University. Her Master's thesis, titled "Race, Gender, and the Problem of 'Ergi' in Modern Heathenry" explored concepts of gender roles within contemporary Heathen ritual structure and their impact on contemporary ideological fault lines. She is currently pursuing a PhD in Classics.

Ms. Krasskova currently writes as a columnist for BBI Media's *Witches and Pagans Magazine,* and she has a variety of published books available running the gamut from introductory texts on the Northern Tradition, runes, prayer, and devotional practices, with more books on the way. She maintains a regular blog at http://krasskova.weebly.com.

Current Publications

Exploring the Northern Tradition (New Page Books)

Northern Tradition for the Solitary Practitioner (with Raven Kaldera, New Page books)

Runes: Theory and Practice (New Page Books)

The Whisperings of Woden (Asphodel Press)

Sigdrifa's Prayer: An Exploration and Exegesis (Asphodel Press)

Feeding the Flame (Asphodel Press)

Root, Stone, and Bone (with Fuensanta Arismendi through Asphodel Press)

Sigyn: Our Lady of the Staying Power (Asphodel Press)

Day Star and Whirling Wheel (Asphodel Press)

Walking Toward Yggdrasil (Asphodel Press)

Full Fathom Five (Asphodel Press)

Into the Great Below (Asphodel Press)

When The Lion Roars (Asphodel Press)

A Child's Eye View of Heathenry (Spero Publishing)

Honoring Sigyn (Spero Publishing)

A Child's Eye View of Divination (forthcoming through Spero Publishing)

Neolithic Shamanism (with Raven Kaldera, forthcoming through Inner Traditions/Destiny Books)

Skalded Apples: A Devotional to Iduna and Bragi (forthcoming through Asphodel Press)